MEGALITHIC MATTERS

MEGALITHIC MATTERS

JOHN R. HOYLE

Matador
9 Priory Business Park
Kibworth Beauchamp
Leicestershire LE8 0RX, UK
Tel: (+44) 116 279 2299
Fax: (+44) 116 279 2277
Email: books@troubador.co.uk
Web: www.troubador.co.uk/matador

ISBN 978 1783062 942

British Library Cataloguing in Publication Data.
A catalogue record for this book is available from the British Library.

Typeset in Aldine401 BT Roman by Troubador Publishing Ltd
Printed and bound in the UK by TJ International, Padstow, Cornwall

Matador is an imprint of Troubador Publishing Ltd

CONTENTS

Introduction   *vi*

1. Some Stone Circles of Mid Wales   1
2. A Search for Possible Megalithic Units of Length   20
3. Megalithic Mathematics   37
4. Prehistoric Remains In Pennal   44
5. Eglwys Gwyddelod. A Possible Lunar Observatory Complex   51
6. Possible Reasons for the Design of Type A and Type B Rings   60
7. Precious Stones. Sources of Stones for Ring Building   68
8. An Alternative to Thom's Design of Avebury   73
9. Other Sites   92
10. Conclusions   101

Index   *105*

INTRODUCTION

Like many people I had taken a general interest in stone circles and had visited Stonehenge and a handful of other rings. Other than wandering round, trying to count the stones and vaguely wondering when and by whom they had been built I did little. They were often in good places to sit and have lunch, so it was usual to sit on one of the stones and admire the view whilst eating a sandwich. This changed when I read the work of Alexander Thom. He saw the rings not as crude structures, but as carefully constructed monuments.

He found that the great majority were circular, but those that were non-circular were set out to carefully designed geometric plans, such as two types of flattened circles, ellipses, egg shaped rings and a few more complex designs. He also claimed that they used a universal unit of length, which he termed the Megalithic Yard. They had also been so well constructed that many had withstood the ravages of time for around four or more thousand years. Intrigued and knowing of several small rings in Mid-Wales, I set out to make accurate surveys of them to see if they conformed to Thom's ideas.

I visited several dozen sites in the process of making these surveys, but found that most of them were in ruins or were just piles of stones and little work could be done. The work though was enjoyable and took me to places that I would not otherwise have gone to. In all this I was greatly helped by my long suffering wife and young children. I am full of admiration for Thom's dedication to his field work. He surveyed several hundred sites, to a very high standard, in all parts of the British Isles, whilst I surveyed about a dozen relatively local ones

Luck can play an important part and I was fortunate in that the rings I surveyed in Mid-Wales had a wide range of types. Only one was circular. Two were flattened circles – one of each type, three were ellipses and two were egg shaped, one of which was unusual in having a normal egg shaped small end and an elliptical big end.

Thom's Megalithic Yard has been the subject of much argument. Thom made a strong case for the unit, but many archaeologists were unconvinced. Because of this I undertook an extended analysis of ring diameters to try to determine which lengths, if any, stood out as possible units. All lengths from 1.5 feet to 15 feet, in steps of one, one thousandth of a foot, were considered. The only length which stood out was the Megalithic Yard, but as this unit did not appear to apply to all groups of rings, I am of the opinion that Thom considerably simplified the situation and evidence for another unit emerged.

New to me at the time was Thom's work on megalithic solar, lunar and stellar observatories. He described the essential characteristics of such structures and as a result, when I searched for them, I knew to some extent what I was looking for. No such megalithic observatory can be expected to be complete and absolute proof of their existence is difficult to find, but there is strong evidence for two lunar observatories within a few miles of my home and tentative evidence for a solar observatory as well.

I have never been happy with Thom's proposed design for Avebury. I have therefore devoted a chapter to an alternative design that is more in keeping with Thom's designs for other non circular rings. The geometrical construction fits the stones at least as well as Thom's and also gives a hint as to why such a design may have been devised, but unless the centres of the arcs can be established by excavation, or other means, it is not possible to prove the correctness of any proposed design.

Often overlooked is the value and importance which large stones must have had for the builders. For large building projects there must have been some form of record keeping and the possibility of using cup and ring marks for this purpose is discussed. The idea is speculative, but the theory makes predictions which may be verifiable. With any scientific theory it is essential that it must not only explain the known facts, but it must also be able to make predictions that are capable of being checked. Such theories are vulnerable to future work or discoveries, but theories that have no predictive ability and can not be disproved, are not really theories at all and can have little or no value.

In Chapter 9 three other sites are described. One is an alignment near Llwyngwril, a second is a possible solar sightline not far from Tywyn in Mid Wales and the third gives an account of the rediscovery of a destroyed ring in Haslingden, Lancashire, where depressions show where stones once stood.

Without a series of coincidences, this book would never have been written. The shape of the Hirnant Cairn Circle did not conform to any of Thom's designs, so I sent him a copy and asked for his comments. He identified it as an egg type ring with an elliptical big end, which was unusual. I replied that if he wished he could use the survey in any way that he wanted and he published it in *Megalithic Remains in Britain and Brittany*. Meanwhile I had contacted *The Royal Commission for Ancient and Historical Monuments in Wales* and was put in touch with Dr. Stephen Briggs. Although perhaps skeptical of some of Thom's ideas, he was most helpful and encouraging and as a result my surveys were published in *Archaeologia Cambrensis* (1984, pp51-63).

I continued to study local sites and develop my ideas but did not do much more, partly because attitudes to Thom's ideas had changed and some classified him with an extreme fringe, making publication more difficult. Then in 2010 my cousin Steven Higgins told me that my survey of the Hirnant Cairn Circle had been republished in *Cracking the Stone Age Code* by Robin Heath, which was a book describing the life and work of Professor Alexander Thom. I contacted Robin Heath and agreed to put all the surveys on his web site, *skyandlandscape.com*, so that they would be accessible to a much wider public.

Only at that stage did I come to the conclusion that the material I had gathered and the ideas that I had developed could perhaps form the basis of a book, which could be of value to others. It would have to be more in the form of a series of papers than a unified whole, but there are themes that are common and permeate the work. Throughout it all my cousin Steven has been encouraging and has supplied lots of information, but in the end I am responsible for the ideas expressed.

Although I have been inspired by Thom, the reader will find that I do not always fully agree with his conclusions. This is not because I believe Thom to be essentially wrong, but because I believe that he oversimplified things. This is particularly true with the Megalithic Yard. Here I think it likely that one other unit was used. If Thom had considered this possibility, which he almost certainly did, he could not discuss it openly until he had convinced the archaeological world of the validity of the Megalithic Yard, which he never did. His problem was that the use of a second unit would reduce the statistical evidence for the Megalithic Yard and thus undermine his arguments, but if he had suggested the use of another unit, his critics would have asked "How many more units are necessary to account for these data?" It was a catch twenty two situation. I believe that Thom made a very strong case for the Megalithic Yard and my surveys and those of other workers have provided strong supporting evidence. Much of this newer evidence comes from non-circular rings, which are probably more recent than the circular ones.

Perhaps then my ideas may help to bridge the gap between Thom's theories and the ideas of more conventional archaeologists. Thom has provided us with a mine of factual information in the form of many hundreds of accurate surveys. It is a pity that it has been underused because of disagreements over his ideas.

CHAPTER 1

SOME STONE CIRCLES OF MID WALES

In the nineteen seventies I became aware of the work of Professor Alexander Thom. Over a prolonged period he had visited and made very accurate surveys of hundreds of stone circles throughout Britain. On the basis of these plans he deduced that these rings were not the crude structures that many believed them to be, but were carefully constructed using a universal unit of length of 2.72 feet, which he called the Megalithic Yard. This unit, he claimed, was used throughout the British Isles and even beyond for a period of a thousand years or more. The rings he believed also conformed to specific designs. Whilst most were circular, some were circles that had been flattened on one side and others were elliptical or egg shaped. The egg shaped rings in particular were made up from circular arcs whose centres lay at the corners of Pythagorean triangles, that is, right angled triangles whose sides were whole numbers of Megalithic Yards. At other remains Thom claimed that stones were arranged so as to indicate solar, lunar and even stellar position and so could act as a calendar and in some cases help to predict eclipses. If Thom's deductions were correct then the implications would be very far reaching. For example, in order to maintain the accuracy of the Megalithic Yard throughout the whole of Britain over such a period, there must have been one body or group of people responsible for the maintenance and standardisation of the unit. This would not have been easy even if metals had been available, but using only wood and stone, it would have been much more difficult. It is not surprising then that many archaeologists did not accept Thom's conclusions.

As I lived in Mid Wales and knew of several stone circles in the area, none of which had been surveyed by Thom, I decided to survey some of them to see if these rings supported his ideas. Over the next ten years or so I visited lots of old cairns, stone circles and other such structures. There were far more of them than I had anticipated, but most were very ruinous, or were just piles of stones with no discernible design. A few though were well enough preserved and had sufficient standing stones, or kerb stones, to enable a meaningful survey to be made. There are undoubtedly many others which would be suitable, but of which I am ignorant.

The surveys were later published in *Archaeologia Cambrensis*, CXXXIII, 1984. The surveys were not exhaustive, nor did they show all there was to be found at any particular site. They concentrated on the positions of the stones at ground level and if the stone was leaning, then the position of the top part was shown dashed.

The surveys were made with the aid of steel or fibre tapes and an astro compass, modified to measure angles to an accuracy of about one quarter of a degree. The accuracy of the surveys of the small rings was about five centimetres or better. For the larger rings the radial errors were about the same, but the errors along the perimeter had somewhat larger values. This was because the astro compass was placed near the centre of the ring, resulting in radial measurements of constant accuracy and perimeter errors which increased with the radius. For the determination of ring geometry, radial measurements are the more important, and therefore the surveys are probably of sufficient accuracy for their purpose.

Having drawn the plan, the Thom type ring geometry that best fitted the stones was then superimposed. Strangely although Tom found that about three quarters of the rings that he surveyed were circular, I found that only one of the rings in my surveys was circular. There appeared to be two flattened circles, one a Type A circle and the other a Type B, three ellipses and two egg shaped rings. One of these, the Hirnant Cairn Circle, was unusual in that the big end was elliptical and not circular. What is not apparent from the individual plans of the rings is the large differences in their sizes. Diagram 1.01 shows all eight rings to the same scale and it is immediately obvious that elliptical and egg shaped rings are very small compared to the circles and flattened circles. The only possible exception here is Bedd Arthur, which is an unusually long and thin ellipse. If, as claimed by Burl, large rings tend to be older than small ones, then it would seem that more complex ring shapes, being small, came rather late in the ring building period. Flattened circles appear to be an exception to this generalization.

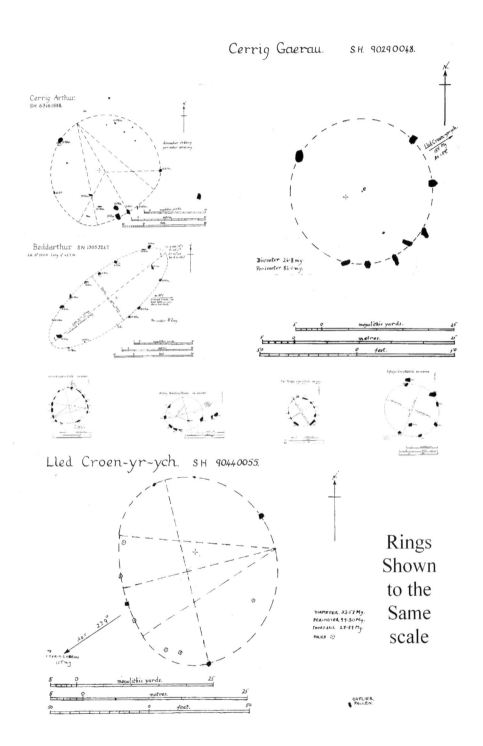

Cerrig Gaerau. S.H. 90290048.

Cerrig Arthur.
SH 63101888.

Beddarthur SN 13053247

Lled Croen-yr-ych. SH 90440055.

Rings
Shown
to the
Same
scale

Diagram 1.01

Plans and descriptions of the individual rings:

CERRIG ARTHUR Grid Reference SH 63161888

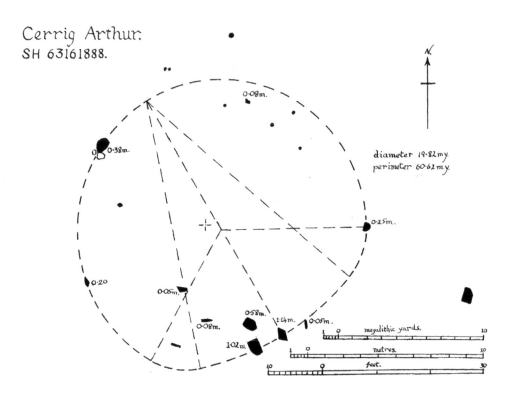

Cerrig Arthur.
SH 63161888.

N

diameter 19·82 m.y.
perimeter 60·62 m.y.

0·08m.

0·38m.

0·25m.

0·20

0·05m.

0·58m.   1·14m.   0·05m.

0·08m.

1·02m.

megalithic yards.

metres.

feet.

Diagram 1.02

CERRIG ARTHUR. LOOKING S.S.E. FROM THE CENTRE. THE HILLSIDE ABOVE
THE LEFT HAND STONE MARKS THE EXTREME SOUTHERLY
RISING POINT OF THE MOON.

J.R.H.

4

The remains of this ring are situated to the north-east of Barmouth and about one quarter of a mile north of the farm called Sylfain. Although there are few stones left standing, the site has been levelled by cutting into the slope on the west side and building up at the east, whilst around the flat area there are traces of a bank. It is therefore quite clear where the ring was originally situated. Five of the stones lie on a Type A flattened circle, with the tallest stone at the south-east end of the axis. One stone of considerable size lies just within the ring and close to the two tallest stones. The fact that the ring has a radius of 9.96 Megalithic Yards and a perimeter of 60.6 Megalithic Yards, together with a correspondence of stones with important geometrical positions, gives confidence in the correctness of the construction. No doubt many of the stones have been used to help build the wall which lies a few yards to the west of the ring. It is probable that excavations would show the original positions of the missing stones and confirm the proposed construction.

The axis of the ring points S.S.E. towards the shoulder of Craig y llyn where the extreme southerly rising of the Moon would have taken place in 1700B.C. There are small notches on the skyline in this area and the O.S. map marks "piles" there as well, which may or may not be significant. The ring has an outlier to the E.S.E.

ARTHOG STANDING STONES
Grid Reference SH 65261393

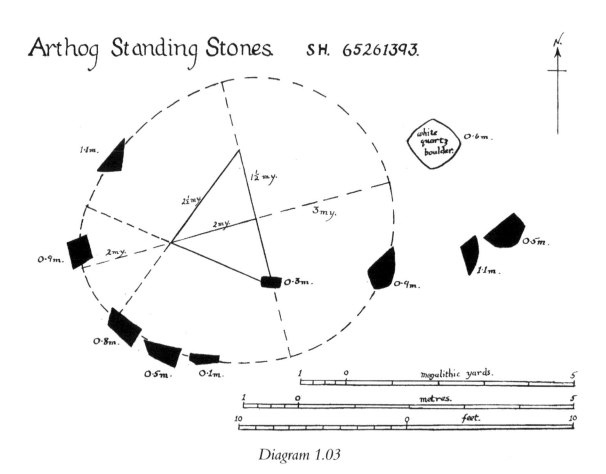

Diagram 1.03

Many of the stones from this ruined ring, or cairn, have no doubt been used to help build the wall that lies to the N.E. of it. Those that remain appear to be rather scattered. It is not possible to construct a ring that passes through all these stones, but if the white quartz boulder and the two standing stones at the east end are ignored, the rest give a near perfect fit on an egg-type ring having all the characteristics proposed by Thom. The basis of the design is a half-size 3, 4, 5, right-angle triangle. The arcs have radii of 2, 3 and 4.5 Megalithic Yards and the perimeter has a value of 20.35 Megalithic Yards. As with the previous ring, excavations would no doubt establish its true geometry and probably throw light on the nature of the stones at the east end the group.

This ring was the first that I surveyed and although I have no reason to doubt the accuracy of the plan, I have less confidence in it than in my later ones. The heights of the stones however were not measured at the time, but estimated later from a drawing and therefore only give an indication of relative heights. The accuracy of the heights of the stones was confirmed on a recent visit to the site.

EGLWYS GWDDELOD
Grid Reference SH 66280018

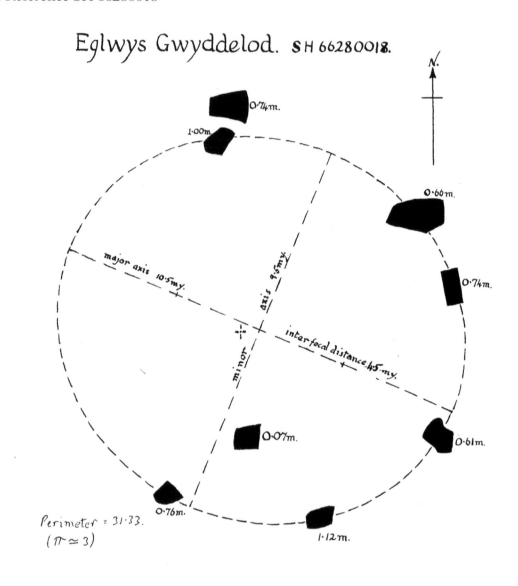

Eglwys Gwyddelod. SH 66280018.

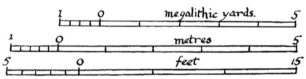

Diagram 1.04

EGLWYS GWYDDELOD   J.R.H.

This small ring is situated between two tracks close to their junction. The stone to the north, outside the ring, is really part of the bank, whilst the large stone to the north east seems to have been displaced to some extent. The centres of the remaining five large stones can be made to fit an ellipse exactly. This is only to be expected, but what is surprising is that the ellipse has a major axis of 10.5 Megalithic Yards, a minor axis of 9.5 Megalithic Yards and a distance between the foci of 4.5 (actually 4.47) Megalithic Yards. The perimeter of 31.3 is not close to a multiple of 2.5, but it is almost exactly three times the major axis.

It is probable that this ring originally had eight stones, but no traces can be seen in the surface of the positions of the other two. (On a later visit it was found that two stones had been placed on the ground on the west side of the ring, presumably to try to complete the ring, but there was no trace of them when the original survey was made.) Although there are no walls very close to this ring, which could have used the stones, local people have told me that early this century (that was the 20th century) the place was used for cock fighting and it is not unlikely that the ring was disturbed during these activities.

CERRIG GAERAU AND LLED CROEN-YR-YCH
Grid References SH 9029 and 90440055

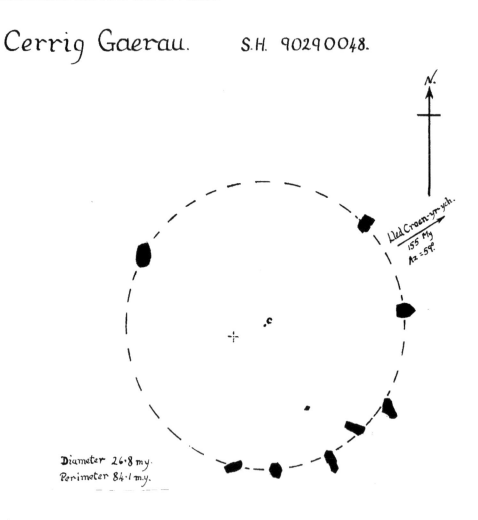

Cerrig Gaerau.   S.H. 90290048.

Diameter 26·8 my.
Perimeter 84·1 m.y.

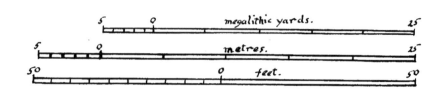

Diagram 1.05

CERRIG GAERAU LOOKING TOWARDS
ARAN FAWDDWY.   J.R.H.

These two rings are situated on a bare hill-top to the south of Llanbrynmair, and to the S.S.W. of them, on the edge of the hill is a ruined cairn. This open site has extensive views in all directions. These rings are the largest of the ones that I surveyed and although quite close together, they are quite distinct in character.

Cerrig Gaerau has eight large stones which Burl states have fallen. This is probably true, but as five of these lie with their centres exactly on a circle and the remaining three are long stones and lie with one of their ends on the same circle, it could be argued that only the last three have fallen and the first five are still in their original positions.

Lled Croen-yr-ych. SH 9044 0055.

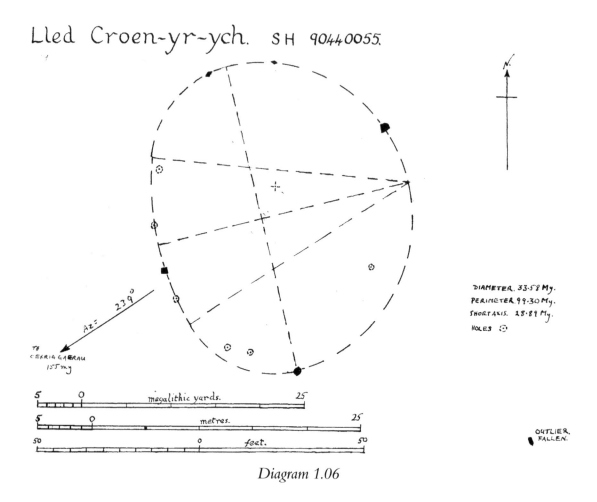

DIAMETER. 33.58 My.
PERIMETER. 99.30 My.
SHORT AXIS. 28.89 My.
HOLES ⊙

OUTLIER.
FALLEN.

Diagram 1.06

About 155 Megalithic Yards (128 metres) to the N.E. lies another ring, Lled Croen-yr-ych, which has 5 rather small stones, and an outlier to the S.E., now fallen. There are also several hollows which may have contained stones in the past, but if so, it is difficult to see what could have happened to them. The ring could well be a Type B flattened circle and the fit is excellent as shown on the plan. However, as there are only five stones, an ellipse can be made to fit just as well. If, though, it was intended to be a Type B ring, the perimeter would be very close indeed to 100 Megalithic Yards.

HIRNANT CAIRN CIRCLE
Grid Reference SN 753839

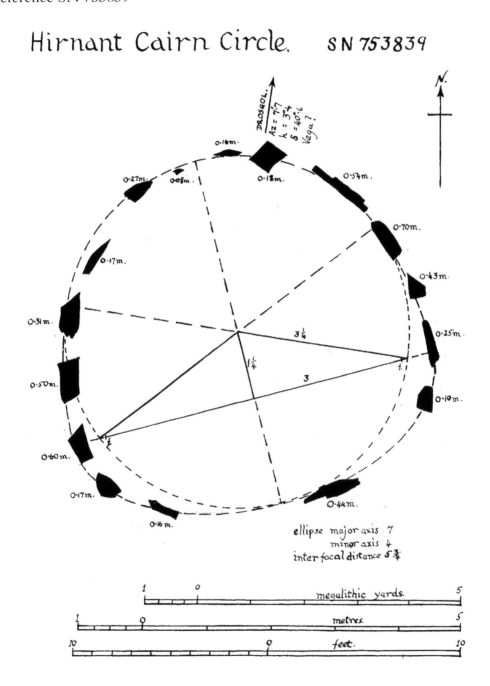

Diagram 1.07

HIRNANT 'CAIRN CIRCLE.

This unusual ring seems to be a combination of an egg-type ring with half of an ellipse. Professor Thom suggested this construction to me and published my first rapid but careful survey in *Megalithic Remains in Britain and Brittany*. This is from a second survey, which involved over two hundred measurements, but differs from the first only in the details of the shape of the stones. For the egg part of the ring (the northern part) I have used a different triangle from that suggested by Thom, but the difference in the shape is minimal.

This ring presents a real problem to anyone who does not accept Thom's ideas of ring geometry. It cannot simply be a badly made circle as it deviates in a symmetrical manner from a circle, so how else can it have been be set out? I. O. Angell (*Angell, Department of Computer Science, Royal Holloway College, private communication.*) suggested that it could have been set out in a manner similar to that for an ellipse, but using three stakes instead of two. The fit was good, but it did not explain why the dimensions were clearly related to the Megalithic Yard.

Since this survey was completed in 1977, the site has become overgrown with rushes and someone has placed two stones in the ring, a large one due south of the centre and a small one to the southeast. These fill gaps and were presumably inserted to try to "improve" the ring. This practice is greatly to be deplored.

THE TEMPLE CAIRN CIRCLE (BWLCH GWYN)
Grid Reference SN 74577917

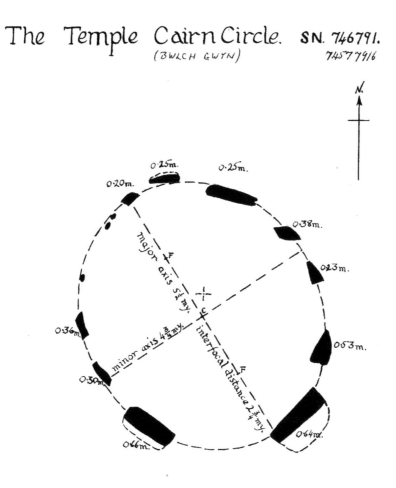

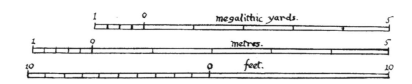

Diagram 1.08

TEMPLE CAIRN CIRCLE   J.R.H.

This very small ellipse only satisfies Thom's conditions if quarter Megalithic Yards are used. This is not very satisfactory, but the dimensions are interesting. The distance between the foci of the ellipse is two and three quarter Megalithic Yards, which is exactly half the long axis. The short axis is four and three quarter Megalithic Yards. The perimeter is almost exactly sixteen Megalithic Yards.

The ring Nine Stones (Winterbourne Abbas) in Dorset has dimensions, given by Thom, (A. Thom, *Megalithic Sites in Britain,* Page 72.) which are exactly twice as great as this ring. In addition both rings have stones which are graded in height. As rings with stones of graded height are not particularly common, the similarity may be more than coincidence. In Nine Stones, the largest stones are at the north, whilst in this ring they are at the south.

BEDD ARTHUR
Grid Reference SN 13053247

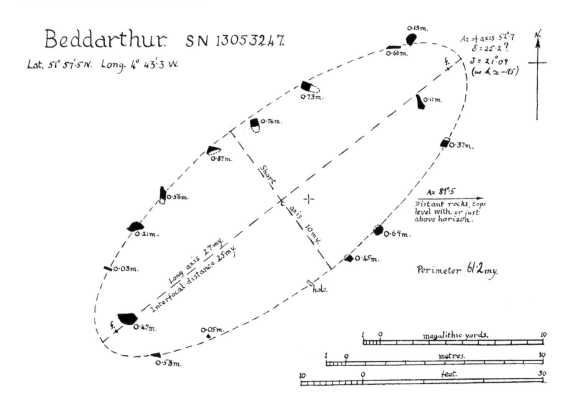

Diagram 1.09

According to the *Pembrokeshire Inventory* (1924) Bedd Arthur is a natural outcrop, and when last surveyed by the O.S. there was general concurrence with this opinion. The site though is clearly not natural and I can only conclude that they have been looking at a rocky outcrop somewhat higher on the hillside. The site has been partially levelled and once seen is obvious, even without the stones.

On the ground the site gives the appearance of a rectangle, but the plan shows that a long ellipse, with all the characteristics required by Thom's theories, passes through, or close to, all the stones but two, and they are on the axis. The major axis, minor axis and interfocal distances are twenty seven, ten and twenty five Megalithic Yards respectively and the perimeter is quite close to sixty Megalithic Yards (actually 61.2).

The stone near the N.E. end of the axis, may once have stood upright on it. If so, it would have indicated a celestial body with a declination of about twenty one degrees when viewed from the other end of the long axis. The stones along the N.W. side lean inwards and this could be due to soil creep down the slope from the higher ground. The same effect could easily have displaced the stones bodily from their original positions.

Modern photographs of this ring appear to show three stones which are not on the above plan. Two of them are in the long gap to the south of the centre of the ring and one is in the gap which is almost due east of the centre. As these stones are of considerable size, it was not possible for me to have missed them when I surveyed the ring in the mid nineteen seventies and the only conclusion I can reach is that someone inserted them to try to improve the appearance of the ring. As mentioned previously, the same has been done at Eglwys Gwyddelod and The Hirnant Cairn Circle and could also have been done at some of the other rings that I have not been able to revisit. Anyone attempting to make accurate surveys of rings should be aware that some of the stones in them may not be old at all and the value of the survey could well be compromised. It is sometimes easy to spot these extra stones, but not always so, and for large stones that have been there for some considerable time, it can be difficult or even impossible to do so without excavation by an experienced person.

The Reverend W. Done Bushell (*Archaeologia Cambrensis* July 1911) stated that there were no upright stones at Bedd Arthur when he visited it, but that the site was unmistakable and had a diameter of about 70ft. If his report is correct, it may be that rebuilding of such rings is not a new practice, but as the stones are not very large, it is possible that he missed seeing them, easily done if they were hidden by clumps of gorse, heather or bracken. It is interesting that he uses different names from the ones shown on modern maps. Carnbica, a rocky outcrop, a short distance to the north west is called by him *Cerrig Marcholion*, which translates as *The Horsemen's Stones* and they do have a passing resemblance to a man on a horse.

CONCLUSIONS

Professor Thom has not surveyed these rings and therefore his conclusions can in no way depend on them. If the Megalithic Yard never existed, why should it fit these rings so well? If it is just luck, it should be possible to select any unit at all, quite at random, and apply that unit to these rings with equal success. For example it should be possible to find equally satisfactory geometrical constructions using the modern yard, or the metre. I have tried to do this, and using the modern yard, I could find Thom type solutions for only three of the eight rings. These were Cerrig Arthur, Eglwys Gwyddelod and Lled Croen-yr-ych, though in the second of the three it was necessary to use quarter units in the interfocal distance. It is possible that I have not explored all possibilities and that other solutions may exist. However, solutions based on the Megalithic Yard have proved easier to find and in some cases it appears to be the natural unit.

It is worth noting that of the fourteen Type A rings listed by Thom, with diameters that range from 37.7 ft. To139.7 ft., two have diameters almost identical to Cerrig Arthur. These are D1/9 and G4/12 with diameters of 54.2 ft. and 54.5 ft. compared with 53.9 ft. for Cerrig Arthur. The Type A rings next nearest in size have diameters either 11 ft. larger or 11ft. smaller, i.e. four Megalithic Yards on either side. Of all the eight rings, the one for which the Megalithic Yard is the least satisfactory is the circular ring Cerrig Gaerau. It is also the crudest looking ring of the group and being large, perhaps the oldest.

CHAPTER 2

A SEARCH FOR POSSIBLE MEGALITHIC UNITS OF LENGTH

The question *"did the builders of megalithic stone circles use an accurate unit of length in their construction?"* is simple. The answer to it is not. Several units have been proposed, but the one which probably has the most backing, is the Megalithic Yard, strongly argued for by Professor Alexander Thom. Thom based his assertion on the basis of the measured diameters of hundreds of stone circles, which he obtained from extremely accurate surveys of their remains. He claimed that the Megalithic Yard was an accurate unit of 2.72 ft. that was used throughout Britain and Brittany for well over one thousand years. He also claimed that the unit was supported by the dimensions of non circular rings, such as ellipses, flattened circles and egg shaped rings. Persuasive though the evidence is, the unit has not gained general acceptance in archaeological circles.

Part of the difficulty lies with the complex and difficult statistical methods used and the suspicion that one length or another could be found that would fit the measured diameters by sheer chance, which is a valid point. To be persuasive, arguments should be clear, straightforward and reasonably easy to understand. Probably Thom's ideas would have been more readily accepted if his conclusions had not seriously conflicted with widely held ideas of the social structures of those times. In general, society was thought by many to be tribal, fragmented and culturally not very advanced. The idea that the people of Britain were mathematically more advanced than the Greeks and had a common culture that ranged from the Shetlands in the north to Brittany in the south, was difficult to accept.

It was with these difficulties in mind that I tried to devise a method for analysing the ring diameter data that would be clear, straightforward and would avoid difficult statistical arguments. However many non-mathematically inclined readers may find some of the following difficult. If so, the difficult parts can be skipped, as they are there to explain how the graphs are produced and it is the graphs themselves that contain the essential information.

This analysis seeks to assess all possible lengths for their suitability as units. The data used are the ring diameters listed by Professor Thom in his book *Megalithic Sites in Britain*, which is probably the most comprehensive and accurate data source available on megalithic ring diameters. There is an infinite number of possible lengths that could be considered as units, but in practice lengths below one and a half feet can be ignored, as the uncertainties in ring diameters are often of this magnitude, and lengths above fifteen feet would be too large to be of much use. There is also no point in considering lengths which are too close together, so lengths were chosen which differed by only 0.001ft. This analysis then covers the range from one and a half feet to fifteen feet in steps of one one thousandth of a foot. (The computer program that I wrote can cover any range of lengths and can have step intervals of any magnitude, but the range covered in this article is probably the most useful.) In all there are about thirteen thousand five hundred lengths covered, which is more than adequate. This paper uses feet as the main unit simply because Thom lists his ring diameters in feet and conversion to metres does tend to give false ideas of accuracy. (For example a ring whose approximate diameter was obtained by pacing and given, say, as 45ft. would appear as 13.7 metres after conversion, giving a misleading illusion of accuracy.)

In order to determine how well a particular length fits a ring diameter, the diameter is divided by that length in order to find the diameter of the ring in multiples of that length. This is then multiplied by 2pi, effectively turning the diameter into an angle in radians (or multiply by 360 if the angle has to be in degrees). The cosine of this angle is then found. The graph beneath illustrates what is happening.

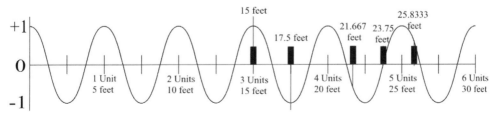

Diagram 2.1

For example, suppose that someone wishes to see if a length of five feet could be a satisfactory unit for rings with diameters of 15ft., 17.5 ft., 21.6667ft., 23.75ft. and 25.8333ft. First divide each diameter by 5 which gives: 3.00, 3.50, 4.333, 4.75 and 5.1667. These are the distances indicated on the diagram by the position of the black rectangles. The height of the curve at the position of the rectangles is the cosine function. These are in turn 1, -1, -0.5, 0 and 0.5. It is easy to see that those diameters which are close to multiples of 5 have cosine functions that are close to +1 and those that lie midway between multiples of 5 have cosine functions which are close to -1. The sum of the cosine functions for this group of rings is zero and this indicates that 5ft. is not a candidate for a unit. In order to be considered as a unit, the sum of the cosine functions should be positive and the more positive it is, the more likely it is for that length to be a unit. For clarity the figures are set out in the table below.

Ring	Diameter in ft.	Diameter in multiples of 5 ft.	Cosine function
1	15.000	3.000	+1.00
2	17.500	3.500	-1.00
3	21.667	4.333	-0.50
4	23.750	4.750	0.00
5	25.833	5.167	+0.50

Sum = 0.00

In the computer program this procedure is carried out for all lengths, from 1.5ft. to 15ft. in steps of 1/1000 ft. in the selected ring group. The sums of the cosines are divided by the square root of the number of rings in the group being examined and the results then plotted on a graph. This procedure is necessary in order to enable direct comparisons of groups with different numbers of rings. If it were not done, groups with larger numbers of rings would tend to produce greater peaks and troughs. The program was written to produce two graphs, one with a linear length scale and the other with a logarithmic scale. The advantage of the latter is that it spreads out the peaks and troughs for the shorter lengths, where they are naturally crowded together. Only the graphs with the logarithmic scale are reproduced in this paper. The amount of calculation is enormous, but a modern desk top computer can do it all in a matter of a second or so, even if the group contains a hundred or more rings.

In order to extract as much useful information as possible, the rings were divided into groups. The more accurate of Thom's ring diameters were split into four groups:

Small English and Welsh – under 50ft	(23 rings)
Large English and Welsh – 50ft. or greater	(22 rings)
Small Scottish – under 50ft.	(35 rings)
Large Scottish – 50ft. or over	(31 rings)

The regional split was made to try to determine if there was a geographical difference between rings and the size split was made because it is believed that smaller rings are, in general, younger than large rings and so it may be possible to detect differences that may have taken place over time. Two other groups were included:

Diameters obtained by Thom, but of lesser accuracy.	(58 rings)
Diameters from other sources but listed by Thom.	(26 rings)

The computer program not only enables all these groups to be studied individually, but allows combined groups such as All Small Rings, All Scottish Rings, All Accurate Rings, etc. In groups with few members the possibility of a particular length appearing to be a good fit by chance, is higher than in a large group, so there are likely to be several peaks which have no significance. In fact the great majority of peaks are there purely by chance. It is also possible that a length that had been used as a unit, may not show up particularly strongly if it had not been widely used. Caution then is needed in the interpretation of these graphs.

RESULTS

A cursory examination of the graphs of Thom's more accurate diameters shows only one peak that stands out. That is for a length of 5.44 ft in the diameters of small Scottish rings. Only a few peaks reach a value of 2, whilst this reaches about 2.6 or 2.7. The graph for the large Scottish rings does not show a corresponding peak, which is strange, as this length is twice the Megalithic Yard and it has often been stated that the evidence for this unit comes mainly from the Scottish rings.

Peaks at about 5.44ft. also occur in the graphs for large English and Welsh rings, Thom's rings of lesser Accuracy, and rings from other sources. When groups are combined this peak tends to increase in height, so that when all the rings are combined the peak reaches a value of 3. This is 25% higher than any other peak and so constitutes strong evidence for this length being a widely used unit. As there are 195 rings in this combined group, the theoretical maximum height the peak could reach is the square root of 195, which is close to 14. If the height of the peak were about half of this, say about 6 or 7, then I believe that all Thom's claims for the Megalithic Yard would have to be accepted without question. As the height is only 3, it may be necessary to modify some of Thom's assertions.

There are several possible reasons why this peak value is not higher.
1) The Megalithic Yard may only have been an approximate unit.
2) The rings may not have been set out accurately or measured accurately.
3) The rings may have been disturbed over the course of time.
4) Some rings may have used an odd number of Megalithic Yards in the diameter.
5) The unit may not have been used for all rings.

Reasons 1, 2 and 3 have been discussed at length on many occasions and it is not proposed to comment further here. The graphs, though may be able to throw light on the last two reasons. The graph for small English and Welsh rings does not have a peak corresponding to 5.44 ft. It does though have a peak at 2.75 ft., which is very close to half of it. This can only be explained by the use of odd multiples of 2.75 ft. in some of the diameters. This would reduce the peak of 5.44 ft. as the cosine function of such rings would be close to -1. Several of the diameters of small English and Welsh rings are in fact close to odd multiples of 2.72ft.

The graph for the large Scottish rings, as mentioned above, is peculiar in that it does not have any evidence for the use of a unit of 5.44ft. Neither are there any other outstanding peaks. There are however peaks close to 2.97 ft. and 4.95 ft. which lie near to our modern yard and five feet. They are just about one percent less. Could it be that an old foot of 0.99 modern feet was used in groups of three and five? I thought that this possibility may be worth further examination. The results of this are quite surprising when applied to some of the megalithic rings. (For ease of writing the unit length of 2.97 ft. will be called the Old Yard or oy.)

Ring of Brodgar

Diameter (Thom)	340.7ft.	125.35my.	114.70oy.
Perimeter	1070.3ft.	393.50my.	360.38oy.

As Brodgar has 60 equally spaced stones, the perimeter in old yards fits extremely well, at 6oy. per stone. The inner rings at Avebury seem to have had the same dimensions as Brodgar.

Sunhoney

Diameter	83.0 ft.	30.51my.	27.95oy.
Perimeter	260.7ft.	95.86my.	87.79oy.

This ring has 11 fairly equally spaced stones so each one is spaced 8oy. from the next, centre to centre.

Castle Rigg. Type A flattened circle. (Perimeter = 3.0591*diameter)

Diameter	107.1ft.	39.38my.	36.06oy.
Perimeter	327.6ft.	120.45my.	110.31oy.
Distance of outlier	296ft.	108.8my.	99.7oy.

This is interesting as the perimeter is both 120my. and 110oy. Could it be that 11oy. equals 12my? The outlier is 100oy. from the centre of the ring, but this result should be viewed with caution, as there is evidence that this stone has been moved closer to a wall and further from the ring. (See chapter on flattened circles.)

The 56 Aubrey holes at Stonehenge form a ring with a diameter of 283.6ft (Thom) and Newham believed that the distance between each third stone, measured along the chord, is an important distance, which he called the Lunar measure.

Diameter	283.6ft.	104.3my.	95.49oy.
Perimeter	890.95ft.	327.55my.	299.99oy.
Lunar measure	47.508ft.	17.466my.	15.996oy.

That the perimeter and Lunar measure should come so close to 300oy. and 16oy. is very surprising to say the least. The old yard was selected as it was a suitable unit for the large Scottish rings and it seems to be the perfect unit for the Aubrey Holes. As will be seen later the old yard is a very satisfactory unit for an alternative geometry of Avebury.

Three rings Farr West (Thom B7/16, 113.2 ft.), Elva plain (Thom L1/2, 113.4 ft.) and Hurlers (Thom S1/1, 113.7 ft.) have almost identical diameters. Their perimeters are close to 120 old yards or 360 old feet. They therefore have dimensions which are one third those of Brodgar.

It is tempting to assume that the Large Scottish rings which showed evidence for use of the Megalithic Yard would not show evidence for the old yard and vice versa. This however is not the case. There is a tendency for rings to show evidence for both units, or none. In the following table the diameters of the large Scottish rings have been given in units of feet, megalithic fathoms (5.44ft.), old yards (2.97ft.) and units of five old feet (4.95ft.). The cosine functions, which indicate how well the units fit, are also listed and if these are greater than 0.50, they are printed in underlined, bold italics. Statistically, one third of the cosines would be expected to be in italics. As there are 31 rings in this group, about ten cosine functions would be expected to be printed in bold italics in each column.

Twelve of the rings are a good fit for the megalithic fathom of 5.44ft., which is not much more than would be expected by chance. Seventeen rings are a good fit for the old yard of 2.97ft. and fifteen are satisfied by the 4.95ft. unit. These numbers are considerably more than would be expected by chance, but as the unit was chosen from the graphs to fit the rings, care must be exercised in drawing conclusions. What is perhaps more significant is that six of the rings satisfy all three units, when only one in 27 would be expected on statistical grounds.

Ring	Diam. Feet	Diam. (5.44ft. unit)	Cosine	Diam. (2.97ft. unit)	Cosine	Diam. (4.95ft. unit)	Cosine
A8/6	54.9	10.09	*0.84*	18.48	-1.00	11.09	*0.84*
B3/7	56.4	10.37	-0.67	18.99	*1.00*	11.39	-0.79
B2/17	56.9	10.46	-0.97	19.16	*0.55*	11.49	-1.00
B1/23	57.0	10.48	-0.99	19.19	-0.36	11.52	-1.00
B7/2	59.1	10.86	*0.66*	19.90	*0.81*	11.94	*0.93*
B2/4	59.2	10.88	*0.74*	19.93	*0.91*	11.96	*0.97*
B2/1	59.3	10.90	*0.81*	19.97	*0.98*	11.98	*0.99*
B6/2	63.0	11.58	-0.87	21.21	0.24	12.27	-0.14
B1/6	64.0	11.76	0.09	21.55	-0.95	12.93	*0.90*
A1/2	65.1	11.97	*0.98*	21.92	*0.87*	13.15	*0.58*
B2/3	66.9	12.30	-0.30	22.53	-0.99	13.52	-1.00
B1/26	67.2	12.35	-0.60	22.63	-0.70	13.58	-0.89
B6/1	68.4	12.57	-0.90	23.03	*0.98*	13.82	0.42
B7/19	69.1	12.70	-0.30	23.27	-0.10	13.96	*0.97*
B2/16	73.3	13.47	-0.99	24.68	-0.43	14.81	0.36
B2/8	74.1	13.62	-0.72	24.95	*0.95*	14.97	*0.98*
B7/18	74.3	13.66	-0.55	25.02	*0.99*	15.01	*1.00*
B3/1	75.1	13.81	0.34	25.29	-0.23	15.17	0.47
B7/12	76.0	13.97	*0.98*	25.59	-0.85	15.35	-0.61
G4/14	82.1	15.09	*0.84*	27.64	-0.62	16.59	-0.86
B7/15	82.9	15.24	0.07	27.91	*0.85*	16.75	-0.02
B2/2	83.2	15.29	-0.27	28.01	*1.00*	16.81	0.36
G4/3	89.1	16.38	-0.72	30.00	*1.00*	18.00	*1.00*
B44	92.0	16.91	*0.85*	30.98	*0.99*	18.59	-0.86
B7/1a	103.9	19.10	*0.81*	34.98	*0.99*	20.99	*1.00*
B7/1b	104.2	19.15	*0.57*	35.08	*0.86*	21.05	*0.95*
B1/8	108.4	19.93	*0.90*	36.50	-1.00	21.90	*0.81*
B5/1	110.0	20.22	0.18	37.04	*0.97*	22.22	0.17
B7/16	113.2	20.81	0.36	38.11	*0.75*	22.87	*0.68*
B7/15	119.9	22.04	*0.97*	40.37	-0.69	24.22	0.17
N1/13	188.3	34.61	-0.75	63.40	-0.81	38.04	*0.97*

It becomes more interesting when perimeters are calculated. For example, with rings B7/1a and B7/1b the perimeters are given below:

B7/1a326.4ft.120.0MY	109.9oy.	65.9(4.95ft units)
B7/1b327.4ft.120.4MY	110.2oy.	66.1(4.95ft units)

These perimeters are virtually exactly 120 Megalithic Yards, 110old yards and 66 five foot units. The only dimensions which are not integral are the diameters when expressed in Megalithic Yards. This, if intentional, was quite a remarkable achievement.

This analysis of ring diameters indicates that Thom's double Megalithic Yard, or fathom of 5.44ft., has considerable support, but in itself it does not prove that it has all the characteristics that Thom ascribed to it. In particular it does not show that it is a highly accurate unit, nor that it was used for all rings. In fact the analysis tends to show that it was not used to any great extent in the large Scottish rings. It was this fact that prompted a search for other units for this group of rings. The length of 2.97ft indicated by the graph, does have support from some individual rings, as also does the length of 4.95ft. If this length were a unit, it suggests that it was in use from a very early date. It then seems to have been used in parallel with the Megalithic Yard before being displaced by it, first in England and Wales and then later in Scotland. The change was probably mostly peaceful. The old yard seems to have been an accurate unit and if it were replaced by the Megalithic Yard, it would have made no sense to have replaced it with a less accurate unit. These ideas are only tentative, but they do appear to fit the facts. It may be that traders from other areas brought in the Megalithic Yard and perhaps the so called Beaker People were responsible. However this is mere conjecture.

If these ideas are correct it follows that in groups of rings, the older rings are more likely to be based on the old yard and the younger rings on the Megalithic Yard. This implies that the northern ring in the hurlers group is the oldest as it appears to be based on the old yard.

It is worth noting that if 12 Megalithic Yards equal 11old yards, as seems to be the case, then as the diameter of the Brogar ring is almost exactly 125 Megalithic Yards and its perimeter is 360 old yards. As the ring has sixty stones, there is one stone for every six old yards in the perimeter. Again, using the above data, the value of Pi can be calculated by dividing the perimeter by the diameter. The perimeter is 360 old yards and the diameter is 125 Megalithic Yards, or 114.5833old yards. (calculated by multiplying 125 by 11 and dividing by 12). The resulting value of 3.141818 is within 0.01% of the true value of Pi and is over five times more accurate than the usual value of 22/7.

OTHER PEAKS

The Small English and Welsh rings have four or five reasonably sized peaks. One peak at 2.75ft. is close to the Megalithic Yard, whilst another at 1.73ft. corresponds to the use of the megalithic fathom (5.44ft) in the perimeter. There are no peaks to suggest the use of a unit of 2.5 Megalithic Yards in the perimeter, as claimed by Thom. This would have shown up as a peak at 2.16ft. This does not necessarily mean that this unit was not used, but simply that this analysis finds no evidence for it in the circular rings.

THE RING OF STENNESS, ORKNEY

This ring appears to be an early one and at its centre there is a square of four long stones, as shown in the following diagram.

Central feature of Stenness

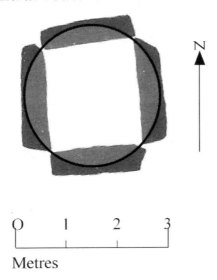

N

0   1   2   3

Metres

Superimposed on it is a circle with a diameter of three old yards, which fits very neatly within the stones.

SUMMING UP

The data from the diameters of the rings listed by Thom support the existence of the Megalithic Yard. It seems to have been used in the radii of all groups except the Small English and Welsh rings, where the graphs suggest that half units were used, and the large Scottish rings, where probably a different unit of 2.97ft, was used. There the basic unit seems to be the old foot of 0.99 modern feet and it seems to have been used in multiples of three and five. If the old yard existed it must have been a highly accurate unit. This follows from the fact that, being a relatively small unit, any errors in the original setting out, or recovery of the diameter from surveys, would very quickly mask its use. An error of only nine inches (0.75ft.) in the measured diameters would essentially hide the evidence for this unit. Also it would seem to have been used at earlier dates than the Megalithic Yard, as it applies to the large Scottish rings, which tend to be older than the small rings and also for the Aubrey hole ring, which is a very early feature of Stonehenge. As there is evidence for the use of the Megalithic Yard in the large English and Welsh rings, but less evidence for its use in the Large Scottish rings, it seems to follow that England and Wales used the Megalithic Yard at an earlier date than Scotland. If the Old Yard were only used in the very early English and Welsh rings, then it is possible that Avebury, as one of the oldest sites, may have used the old yard. This could throw some doubt on Thom's proposed design for Avebury.

Much of Thom's evidence for the Megalithic Yard comes from non-circular rings. It would have been possible to include a consideration of flattened circles, but apart from a graph, they have been excluded, even though they tend to support the unit. Clearly much work remains to be done, but the possibility of a new – or old – unit could stimulate new thinking on the subject of megalithic units of length.

Graphs of suitability of units for different groups of rings.
All units tested from 1.5ft. to 15ft. in steps of .001ft.

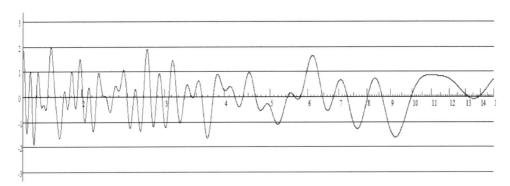

Accurate English and Welsh Small

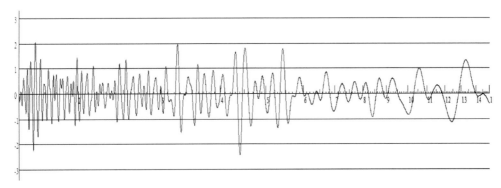

Accurate English and Welsh Large

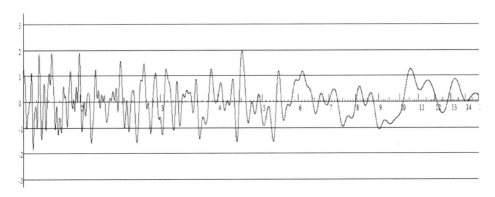

All Accurate English and Welsh

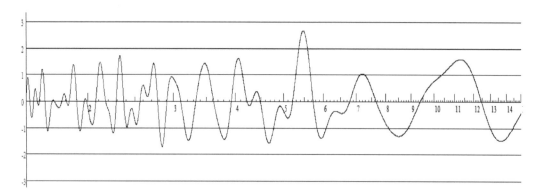

Accurate Scottish Small

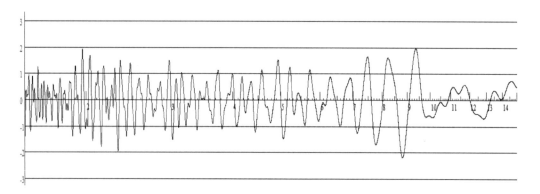

Accurate Scottish Large

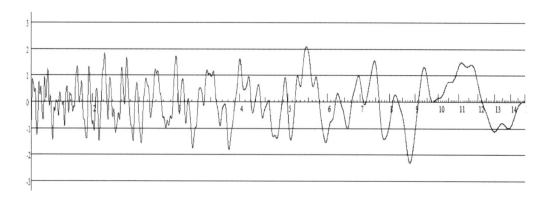

All Accurate Scottish

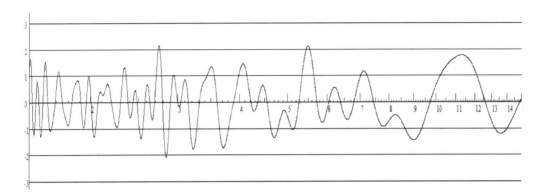

All Accurate Small

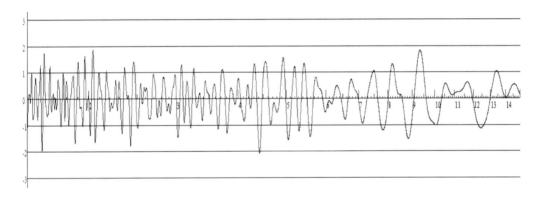

All Accurate Large

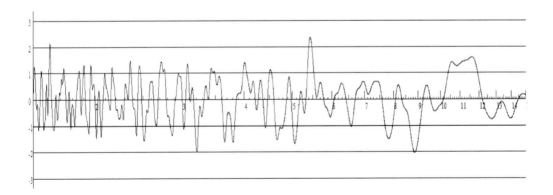

All Accurate Rings

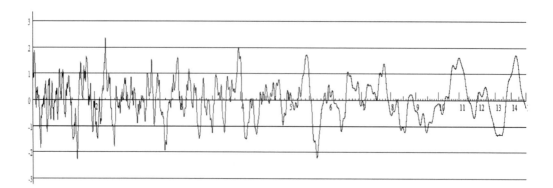

Rings With Less Accurate Diameters

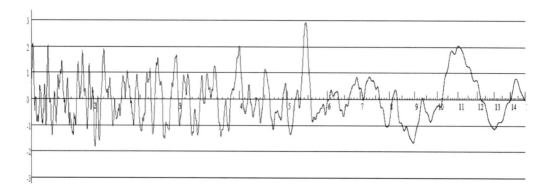

All Thom's circular Rings

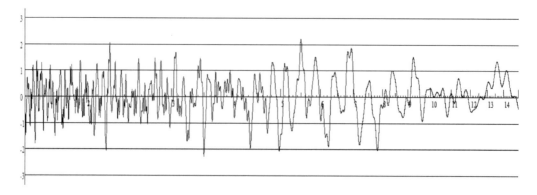

Circular Rings From Other Sources

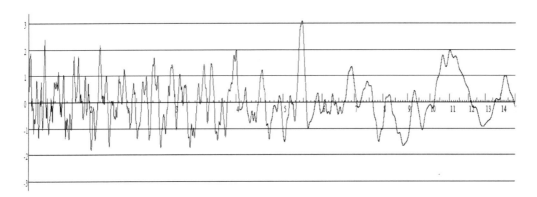

Every Circular ring

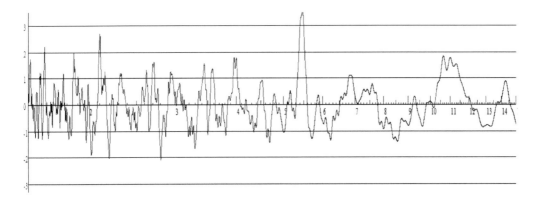

All Circular Groups Except Large Scottish and Small English and Welsh

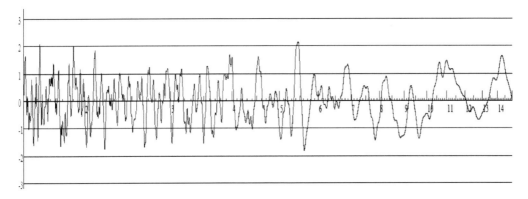

All Rings Except Small Scottish

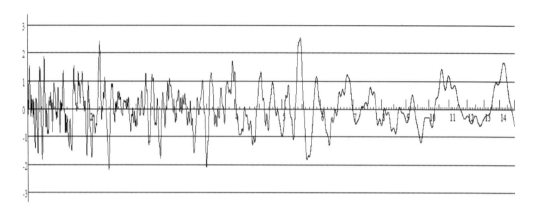

All Rings Except Small English and Welsh, Large Scottish and Small Scottish.

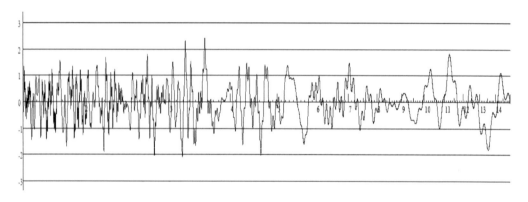

Non-circular rings (Type A and B flattened circles)

CHAPTER 3

MEGALITHIC MATHEMATICS

In 1913 the English mathematician G. H. Hardy received a letter from Srinivasa Ramanujan, a young man from a poor family in India. The letter contained details of some of Ramanujan's own mathematical researches and several proofs of mathematical theorems, many of which were entirely new. Hardy was so impressed with the work that he invited Ramanujan to England and although reluctant, Ramanujan eventually came to continue his researches and became a good friend of Hardy. The remarkable thing about Ramanujan, was that he had had little or no formal mathematical education and his parents had been unable to help – his father worked as a clerk in a sari shop and his mother was a housewife and sang in a local temple. He learned his mathematics from books that he managed to get, or was given, and then his own natural abilities carried him on. Hardy believed that he was one of the greatest mathematicians of all time, comparable with Euler and Gauss.

Throughout human history, there have been small numbers of highly gifted people, not only in mathematics, but in music, art and other fields, whose abilities appeared to be innate and who stood head and shoulders above their contemporaries. Ramanujan was an extreme example of this, but he was not the only one and in prehistoric times, even though populations were small, there must have been a few people with great gifts. Unfortunately, in many societies, these gifts would have gone unrecognized and perhaps the person would have been thought of as rather odd, but if these talents were valued by society then such people could have been highly regarded and selected for promotion to positions of importance.

In any society that regarded the heavens and particularly eclipses, with awe and wished to predict them, there would be a desire to find people with the necessary talents to solve this forecasting problem and those people with high intelligence and mathematical ability would be in considerable demand. Clearly such people could only work with the tools that were available to them, but many of the tasks, such as counting the days between repeating celestial phenomena, although not difficult, demanded accurate record keeping. They would, for example be able to count the days in the year, the days from full Moon to full Moon, and try to work out the number of years that equated to a whole number of lunar months, so as to try and find out the length of cycles when celestial events repeated themselves. To do this they would need to mark in some way the extreme rising and setting points of the Sun to determine fixed points in the year. None of this is conceptually difficult, but it requires care and dedication over long periods. No eclipse prediction is possible though without studying the motions of the Moon and here they would have encountered greater problems, as the movements of the Moon are much more complex than those of the Sun. However, once embarked on this line of research and with sufficient patience, it is inevitable that the 18.6 year cycle that determines the extreme setting points of the Moon would be discovered.

Any knowledge gained would be passed down and from time to time some more gifted person would discover new and better methods for achieving their ends. If Thom is correct the process went on for a thousand years or more, so there was more than adequate time to find and recruit a considerable number of highly gifted individuals. Because the time scales for the Solar and Lunar cycles were so long, the observers could only have taken measurements for a few cycles and it would have been necessary to mark the various sightlines in a substantial manner perhaps with large stones to be used in conjunction with distant hill slopes or other features, and pass on their knowledge to other observers. In remote areas some of these remains could be expected to survive to the present time and these are what Thom claimed to have found.

Some people have criticised Thom because they have concluded that Thom's theories imply that prehistoric man had a deep understanding of Mathematics and Astronomy. Undoubtedly a few people had these gifts, but most did not. The actual degree of mathematical expertise required to operate some of the observatories was limited to marking the point from which the rising or setting of the Sun or Moon could be seen behind a distant foresight, making a note of the spot and measuring the distance of this spot from another fixed point. This procedure was done on consecutive nights. In the case of the Sun this was all that was necessary to find the extreme rising or setting points. In the case of the Moon other procedures had to be carried out to extrapolate to the extreme rising or setting points. The theory of these processes is not simple and the persons responsible for designing the observatories must have had considerable insight into the problem, but the observatories were constructed in such a way that in practice the operator only needed to follow a simple set of rules to obtain the desired results.

For the few who had mathematical abilities, numbers and the relationships between them would be of utmost importance. Numbers were perhaps seen as the key to understanding the Universe and if so they would not be unlike cosmologists today. The difference is that they were just starting on this process of discovery, whilst today we have made huge strides in our understanding of everything from the smallest particles to the vastness of space and the galaxies within it, but in spite of that, the ultimate goal of a theory of everything appears tantalisingly just out of reach and perhaps it will always remain so. The understanding we do have, whether of quantum theory or of relativity, depends on mathematics and mathematics of the most difficult kinds. The machines that are necessary to perform the experiments are the most complex and accurate ever built, ranging from huge telescopes on high mountain tops, with mirrors that flex to compensate for shimmering of the atmosphere, or else placed in space and operated remotely to avoid atmospheric problems altogether, to the huge particle accelerators such as the Large Hadron Collider, buried deep underground in a twenty seven kilometre long circular tunnel. Much of this machine is cooled in liquid helium to allow the magnet coils to be superconducting and produce much stronger magnetic fields. The particle detectors record and analyse unimaginable quantities of data from the shattered remnants of the particle collisions. The costs of these machines are so great that countries have to cooperate to find the necessary finances. The builders of Avebury, Stonehenge and some of the other large monuments must have put in an equal proportion of their limited resources, or perhaps even more, which indicates how important these projects were to the local populations.

We do not know what stone-age man believed. Thom held that some of the remains were lunar or solar observatories and they would have worked well as such. Thom's interpretation of the stone fans of Caithness as devices for extrapolating to find the extreme rising or setting points of the Moon fits the facts well and is a very practical method for achieving this end. However it does not seem likely that all the remains had a practical use. In particular, stone rings designed as flattened circles, ellipses or compound rings do not seem to have had any practical use. It seems that in these cases the designs incorporated some mathematical relationship, such as a Pythagorean triangle or perhaps some way of relating the perimeter of the ring to the diameters. These concepts would have had more of a mystical or perhaps religious nature. Were they perhaps striving for some form of perfection? Did they believe that perfect mathematical relationships, such as the three-four-five right angled triangle, hinted that there was something beyond their everyday world that was pure and perfect and that the study of numbers was the way to discover this perfection? Did they believe that rings incorporating these relationships had special or even magical properties? Without written records we can not know, but the designs of many of these rings suggests that this, or something similar, may have been the case.

Seven of the rings that Thom surveyed had egg shapes and the stones were arranged on circular arcs with different radii. He then discovered that the centres of these arcs lay at the corners of right angled triangles, whose sides were integral, or half integral, numbers of Megalithic Yards. All the egg shaped rings had different designs, but all were based on such right angled triangles. Some archaeologists were unconvinced and argued that, as many of the rings were rather ruinous, the designs had been made to fit the rings and that any connection with the supposed Megalithic Yard was spurious. Others argued that there were other ways of designing such rings, such as placing three pegs in the ground and using a loose loop of rope around them to guide a stake, which could then scribe a ring with the approximate shape of the stones. This method is similar to that used for drawing ellipses, but using three, or possibly four, stakes instead of two. No explanations were given for the choice of positions for the three stakes, or the length of the loop of rope, or of why the dimensions were clearly linked to the Megalithic Yard. The method is possible, but it raises far more questions than it answers.

Two of my own surveys support Thom's thesis. The Arthog Standing Stones, although not as complete as one would wish, does conform very accurately to one of Thom's Type

1 egg shaped rings and uses a half size 3,4,5 triangle. The diminutive but extremely well preserved ring, the Hirnant Cairn Circle, is egg shaped with a difference. The Egg part of the ring is based of quarter size 5,12,13 triangle, whilst that elliptical part has dimensions:

Major axis	7my.
Minor axis	4my
Inter focal distance	5.7445my (Very close to 5.75my)

With these dimensions the foci of the ellipse lie close to the basic circle and the ellipse touches this circle tangentially. The design is aesthetically satisfying and it raises the question as to why such an intriguing design was only used to make a very small ring. Perhaps the answer is that although the dimensions of the elliptical part are very nearly integral in quarter Megalithic Yards, the foci do not quite lie on the perimeter of the basic circle, being about 10 cm. (0.122 my.) inside it.

Since Thom did his surveys, other people have searched and found other similar examples of egg shaped rings, such as a Type 1 Egg on Lundy Isle, that was surveyed by Robin Heath. The evidence Thom produced for the incorporation of Pythagorean triangles in the designs of egg shaped rings was very strong and over the years it has become much stronger as independent workers have found new examples. It is not unreasonable then to consider how much understanding of geometry these early people had.

Two aspects of geometry would have been of particular interest to them. Firstly the evidence indicates that they were concerned with finding right angled triangles with integral sides and secondly there was the practical problem of setting out arcs with long radii as at Avebury. Two of the arcs at Avebury have radii of over one quarter of a mile. It is obvious that measuring accurately from the centre of the circle to points on the arc would have been an exceptionally difficult and tedious task. It certainly could not have been done satisfactorily with a rope due to stretching and it is certain that consideration would have been given to other possible methods of setting out these arcs.

The problem is illustrated in the following diagram (not to scale).

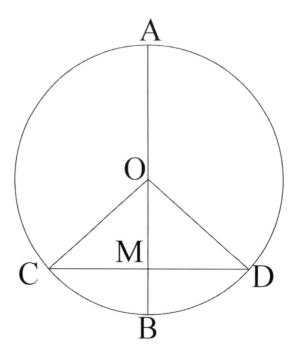

Diagram 3.1

M is the mid point of the chord CD and MB is called the sagitta. The aim was to set out an arc CBD with a centre O. It is quite clear that MB must be less than MD and MC, which are equal, and MA is longer than any of them. By intuition, or measurement, it would not have been too difficult to reach the conclusion that AM times MB equals MC times MD or MD squared. This is true and is a particular example of the theorem of the products of portions of intersecting chords. Using this relationship it would have been possible, using the chord length and the radius of the ring, to calculate the sagitta MB and so locate the centre point of the arc. Other points could then have been found in a similar manner and the whole arc set out accurately without even going to the centre O. The mathematically inclined reader may note a problem here. The solution to this problem results in a quadratic equation, which would probably have caused difficulties. However if the arc was fairly flat, the square of MD could be divided by the diameter AB and this would have given an approximation to the value of the sagitta. Dividing the square of MD by the diameter less the approximate value of the sagitta, would have given a much improved value of the sagitta and repeating this process would very quickly have reduced the errors to negligible amounts. These processes required an ability to add, subtract, multiply and divide, which would have been well within the abilities of the more mathematically gifted members of the Neolithic population.

Neolithic man could also have used the above ideas in reverse in order to find Pythagorean triangles. As an example suppose the length of a chord CD was 14. Half of the chord would be 7 and its square 49. As 1 x 49 equals 49 it follows that if AM were 49 then MB would be 1. The diameter of the circle would be 50 and its radius 25. From the above diagram is seen that the distance OM is 24. So the triangle DMO has sides of 7, 24 and 25, which in fact is a perfect Pythagorean triangle. Any number, in fact all, Pythagorean triangles can be discovered by this process and the method was well within the abilities of the ring builders.

Probably geometrical knowledge of triangles would initially have resulted from the practical aspects of building huts and other structures and only later refined by more accurate measurements. It would have been an empirical process. At some stage though, more rational and inductive processes would have been developed, though there is no evidence for the development of a geometrical system based on a few self evident postulates such as that set out in Euclid's geometrical system. As some of the triangles used were not perfect Pythagorean triangles, but only very good approximations to them, it would seem that they were prepared to use results that were not absolutely perfect.

CHAPTER 4

PREHISTORIC REMAINS IN PENNAL

The casual traveler through Pennal can not help noticing the wall of the churchyard as this roughly circular feature of the village slows the traffic and results in two nasty bends. It has been suggested that it has this shape because the church was built on a much older ritual site of this shape in order to Christianise it. This belief could well be correct, as the first church on this site was believed to have been established in 1087 A.D. and so is very old. Another local tradition has it that the churchyard was made circular so that the Devil would have no corners to hide in. The wall at the south side of the church however is not in its original position, as it has been moved at least twice in order to widen the road. The wall on the north side though may well be in its original position and there are large stones built into its base, one or two of which are of white quartz.

To the south east of Pennal are the remains of a Roman fort, Cefn Caer, which demonstrates the importance of the area, being close to the estuary of the river Dyfi where it is still navigable. To the west south-west of Pennal and south of the main road is a tree covered mound Tomen Las. A local tradition relates that it was built so that Owain Glyndwr could stand on the top of it and speak to the people, but as this flat topped mound has a diameter of about thirty two metres and is four and a half metres high, it is somewhat excessive for that purpose. To put it in perspective, the mound must weigh about five thousand tons and, assuming that a man could have placed ten tons of earth on the mound each day, it would have taken fifty men ten days to build. In addition these men would have had to be supplied with food, drink and tools, so the total workforce must have been considerably greater. What is more likely is that, if Owain Glyndwr did speak from the mound, he stood on a mound that was already there.

It is also known that in medieval times mounds such as this were used as lookout posts to watch over the estates and prevent theft. Again the mound seems to be excessively large for such a use and it would have been much easier to have had the lookout stationed on higher land close by.

Two versions of a more colourful story are related in *Archaeologia Cambrensis, 1885* (page 24) and 1886 (pages 542-543). They describe how a certain Thomas apGriffiths killed a man called David Gough in a sword fight. Thomas, having been injured, lay face down to recover, and was himself killed by one of David Gough's followers, who crept up on him. Thomas apGriffiths was then buried and the mound built over him. Again, if there is some truth in the story, it is probable that he was buried under an existing mound.

There have been suggestions that the mound was built for defensive purposes, but here there is the opposite problem, the mound is far too small for effective defence and the positioning of it is totally unsuitable, being on low flat ground, where attackers could shower the crowded defenders with arrows from all sides. The previously mentioned Roman fort to the south east of Pennal, was on higher land and was far easier to defend.

To the north of Tomen Las and across the road from it is a slightly smaller but otherwise similar tree covered mound. This does not seem to have a name and there do not appear to be any stories or traditions associated with it. This seems rather strange as this tumulus is comparable in shape and size to Tomen Las and it would seem reasonable to assume that the two are connected in some way and should perhaps be treated as a pair.

As these mounds appear to be old they could be Neolithic and it seemed appropriate to consider their possible use as a lunar observatory, as described by Professor A. Thom. The two mounds could act as backsights in conjunction with a cairn on top of Pen Carreg Gopa, which would act as the foresight. Older OS maps do not show a cairn at this position, whilst more recent ones mark it as "Cairn" rather than "𝕮𝖆𝖎𝖗𝖓", indicating that it is not considered old. A visit to the site showed however that the cairn had fairly recently been rebuilt from the remains of a very much older, but unobtrusive cairn, whose diameter was about ten metres and some of the old stones lie scattered about. The new cairn is about two metres high and three metres in diameter and is certainly much more obvious than the old one. That probably explains the changes in the OS maps.

A second cairn on the summit of Foel Goch (GR SN 69515 92850) is visible from Tomen Las, but as this is due south, it is unlikely to have any astronomical significance. A cairn is marked on the O.S. maps with a grid reference of SN764943, but a visit to it showed that it was a natural feature resulting from the projection of very steeply inclined strata. Older O.S. maps have the word "Cairns" in this position and there are in fact several such near vertical outcrops in the vicinity. As the Pen Carreg Gopa cairn marks the only acceptable foresight between south and east, it avoids the problem of selection. Calculations of the declinations indicated by this cairn, when viewed from the two mounds would indicate whether or not they were significant Solar or Lunar declinations. These calculations soon showed that the Sun could never have risen as far south as the cairn, but that the Moon would have risen close to the cairn when it had its extreme southerly declination.

The following results were the best that I could obtain using O.S. maps and an online program to obtain more accurate grid references. The declinations were calculated using mean lunar parallax and refraction data obtained from *Megalithic Lunar Observatories* by A. Thom. The results given below include the declination as seen from the Church as well as those from the tumuli. It is clearly not ideal to use the church as a backsight without other supporting evidence but there are some indications that it was so used. As already stated, it is known that some churches were built on pre-Christian sites and this may be the case here. Perhaps more importantly, the line joining the church to Tomen Las and the line joining the centre of this line to the Pen Carreg Gopa cairn are exactly at right angles. The layout is shown in the following map.

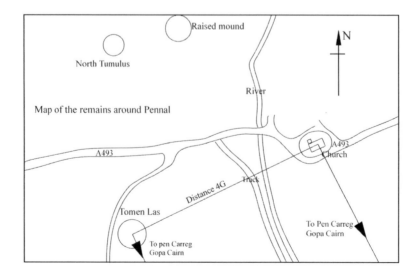

Declinations calculated for Pen Carreg Gopa (GR SN 72152 94775) as seen from the following backsights, using map data.

Centre of Church	-29.341 degrees
North Tumulus	-28.906 degrees
Tomen Las	-28.466 degrees
Raised moundAbout	-29.0 degrees

There is a small but not inconsiderable range of possible rising points for the Moon when it is close to its extreme declination. The main factors which affect the exact rising point are:

(a) the limb of the Moon being observed,
(b) lunar parallax, which depends on the distance of the Moon from the Earth,
(c) a small perturbation, which varies with the relative positions of the Sun and Moon.
    This perturbation is indicated by d in the following tables.
(d) the time difference between the maximum declination and the time of moonrise.

The possible declinations are listed below using mean parallax.
Extreme southerly declinations in degrees.

Plus d		-28.692
Upper limb (+s)	-28.815	
Minus d		-28.938
Moon centre (-e-i)	-29.074	
Plus d		-29.210
Lower limb (-s)	-29.333	
Minus d		-29.456

Declination of Moon one lunar day before or after maximum.

Plus d		-27.917
Upper limb (+s)	-28.040	
Minus d		-28.163
Moon Centre (-e-i)	-28.299	
Plus d		-28.435
Lower limb (-s)	-28.558	
Minus d		-28.681

The data used to calculate the above declinations are listed below.

Inclination of the Earth's axis in 2000BC	(e)	23.929 degrees
Mean tilt of Moon's orbit	(i)	5.145 degrees
Semidiameter of Moon (mean)	(s)	0.259 degrees
Perturbation in inclination of Moons orbit.	(d)	0.123 degrees
Change in declination of Moon one day from max.		0.775 degrees

The inclination of the Earth's axis (e) is slowly decreasing by about one hundredth of a degree per hundred years. This is so small that it is unlikely to have much effect on the above results unless the observatory had been in use several hundred years before or after 2000B.C. The Pen Carreg Gopa cairn is not quite on the highest point of the hill but situated a little to the left. If it had been built on the top then the observatory would have been suitable for observations around 3000BC. It is possible then that the cairn could have been moved to allow for the change in tilt of the Earth's axis.

The Pen Carreg Gopa cairn, when seen from the centre of the church indicates a declination close to -29.341 degrees, which corresponds to the lower limb of the Moon when it has maximum southerly declination. Under the same conditions the declination of -28.906 as seen from the North Tumulus would closely correspond to the upper limb. Tomen Las with an indicated declination of -28.466 best fits observations for the lower limb one day before or after maximum declination. The above map of the area shows an indistinct low mound to the north east of the northern tumulus. Using this as a backsight it would indicate the declination corresponding to the centre of the Moon as it rose with extreme southerly declination. The distance from the church centre to Tomen Las is very close to 300 metres and the calculated value of the theoretical distance, which Thom called 4G, is 304 metres, which is very close. This site then has everything that is required for a megalithic lunar observatory. Unusually, there was here the ability to observe both the upper and lower limbs of the Moon at the same time and this would enable the observers to obtain some information on the apparent diameter of the Moon and hence its relative distance from the Earth and perhaps even its relation to parallax. The following photograph and diagrams give some idea of what could have been observed around 2000B.C. The diagrams are for guidance only.

The Pen Carreg Gopa cairn as seen from Tomen Las

Extreme southerly Moonrise over Pen Carreg Gopa cairn:

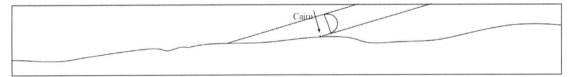

As seen from seen from Pennal Church.

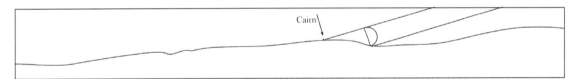

As seen from the North Tumulus.

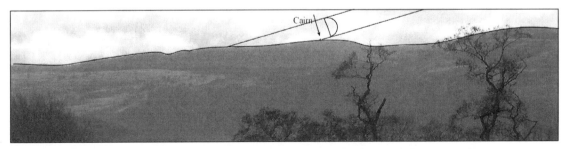

Moon as seen from Tomen Las, rising exactly one day before or after it reaches its extreme southerly declination

It must be stressed that these results are the best that could be obtained from maps, but the calculated declinations may have errors of a few tenths of a degree. I believe therefore that the results should be checked by direct measurement using a theodolite.

It is remarkable that all possible megalithic features in the area, in conjunction with the only cairn visible between south and east, give valid lunar sightlines. There is no ambiguity and nothing is superfluous. The land around is flat and eminently suitable for making the necessary observations. The cairn is high on the hilltop and in good visibility observations of moonrise could probably be made in daylight before the sun had set. My own observations indicate that this would have been possible. In my view it is difficult to argue that this was not a lunar observatory and the site is worthy of more detailed investigation.

CHAPTER 5

EGLWYS GWYDDELOD
A POSSIBLE LUNAR OBSERVATORY COMPLEX

DESCRIPTION

Few of the hundreds of walkers on the old coach road from Pennal to the Dysynni Valley raise their eyes and notice the diminutive stone ring of Eglwys Gwyddelod, nestling on a small platform, thirty or so paces above them. The few that do see it usually spend a few minutes looking round and then rejoin the track. It is a pleasant spot, but not exciting. The stones are half hidden by the rushes that grow in clumps around them. It has not always been like this. A hundred years or so ago, it would, from time to time, have resounded to excited shouts and sounds of cockfighting, as locals wagered their cash on the outcome of these contests. The approach of the law was signaled by lookouts and the crowd would have melted away, leaving nothing but blood and feathers. That time has passed, but the meetings were remembered and recounted to me by one of the older men of Tywyn.

Around four thousand years ago quite different activities took place around this ring, activities whose nature we can now only guess at. That it was a ceremonial centre is easy to accept, but what the nature of these ceremonies was is much harder to answer and we can probably only get hints of what took place. There are however clues, not so much in the ring itself as in the surroundings. These clues are not obvious and I had been to the ring dozens of times before I noticed them and put together some sort of picture. Without the work of Professor A. Thom, I would never have become aware of what to me, now seems clear and without the work of Professor C. Ruggles on the North Mull Project, I would have found it more difficult to derive a convincing argument for these ideas.

SITE AND SIGHTLINE DESCRIPTIONS

About ten metres to the North of this ring there is a shallow depression or groove that runs diagonally across and up the hillside, in a roughly Northeast direction. It acts as a track, but it is not unlike some of the small opencast metal mine trials that follow the line of a mineralized vein. There are however, no obvious signs of spoil heaps and it looks to be much, much older than other such trial excavations which occur in this area. About seventeen metres up this groove, or track, the right hand side is pierced by a cutting, which breaks through to the lower slope of the hillside. It is only a metre wide at the base and a few metres long and appears to have no use at all. A further twenty metres further up the track another track joins it from the west. This track gradually diverges from the lower track and climbs gently up and across the hillside for some time before levelling out beyond and above the stone circle. About 110 metres from the junction it gradually loses itself in the hillside, not far from a ruined cairn. The part of this track overlooking the short cutting seems to have been built up to form a low platform. The following map illustrates the layout of the site.

Sketch map of Eglwys Gwyddelod and Area

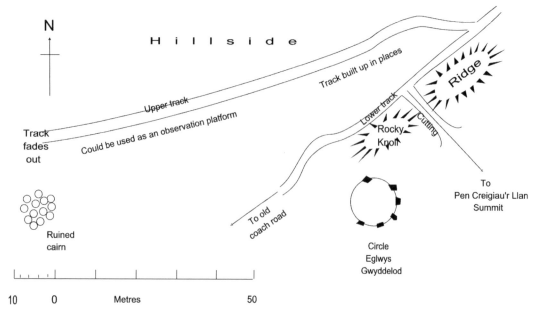

The views from many stone circles are often wide and extensive. That is not the case with Eglwys Gwyddelod, as a low hill to the South restricts the outlook in that direction, though Pennal village and the tumulus Tomen Las, can be seen to the East. On walking up the lower track, the mountains of Central Wales begin to come into view, and by the time the junction with the other track is reached, almost all these mountains can be seen in a wide panorama and most remain visible from all parts of the upper track. Apart from Pumlumon Fawr, the highest visible mountain in this part of Wales, there is nothing obvious along the rest of the skyline that I had noticed and that could act as a foresight for an astronomical sightline and I had looked for one on many occasions.

From the lower track, at the point opposite the side cutting, a nondescript hill top comes into view. A metre below the cutting it is not visible. A metre above the cutting it is. The fact that this unprepossessing knoll comes into view, at the exact point on the track which is opposite the cutting, made me curious. This arrangement gives the distinct impression that it was intentional and intended to indicate the knoll. The hill is Pen Creigiau'r Llan and the declination of a celestial body rising behind it would be close to -19.91degrees, or if lunar and allowing for mean lunar parallax -19.10 degrees. In 1900B.C. the obliquity of the ecliptic was 23.92 degrees, the tilt of lunar orbit 5.15 degrees and the semi diameter of the Moon 0.26 degrees (at the mean distance and parallax). The extreme southerly declination of the lower limb of the Moon at the time of the minor standstill is given then by:

$$- (23.92 - 5.15 + .26) = -19.03$$

As this is very close to the observed declination of -19.10degrees, it would seem that this site could have been chosen for observing moonrise at that time. Under these conditions the Moon would have been seen rising with its lower limb just grazing the knoll.

There is another possible astronomical sightline visible from the platform and the rest of the upper track. Midwinter sunrise would have taken place over Pumlumon Fawr whose summit cairn gives a declination of -24.28 degrees when seen from the platform. The sunrise would be difficult to observe as the lower limb of the Sun would graze the cairn and as the Sun would be in full view it would be too bright to look at safely. Until an accurate skyline profile has been constructed, it is not possible to determine where the first glimpse of the Sun would have been seen.

SIGHTLINES

There is no doubt that the visibility of the knoll from the track in conjunction with the cutting, accurately and unambiguously identifies the knoll, but the question remains: is this accidental, or intentional? The degree of accuracy in indicating this hill top is such, that it is difficult to believe that it was not intended. To me though the method appeared strange and I had nagging doubts. Later I read of the work of Professor C. Ruggles on some of the stone age monuments in North Mull. Here he discovered similar methods being used. Features were indicated by being on the limit of visibility. A small movement in one direction would hide the feature completely and a small movement in the opposite direction would reveal it. It is worth quoting from Ruggles account.

C. Ruggles (*Astronomy in Prehistoric Britain and Ireland*. Page 123. Yale University 1999)
"A question of considerable interest is what might have been the reason for constructing a monument in a place from which a prominent peak – a sacred hill or mountain, perhaps – or a special astronomical event, again possibly of great sacred significance, was on the very limit of visibility? Why should it not be easily visible from all around the monument?"

Here in Mid Wales, unlike North Mull, there is no prominent peak in the indicated direction, only a distant rocky knoll that barely protrudes above the rest of the horizon, so it is probable that this indicator can only be for a special astronomical event. If this interpretation is correct then an important point needs to be taken into consideration. That is that the foresight of a sightline may not be at all obvious and can be easily missed, as I had previously done. In fact the only criterion for a sightline is that a suitably trained person could have successfully identified and used it at the time. It should come of no surprise that people who are not so trained and who and are not certain about what they are looking for, do not find anything. The application of any criteria which do not take these facts into account risk missing the essentials. Ruggles clearly appreciated this fact and states:

C. Ruggles (*Astronomy in Prehistoric Britain and Ireland*. Page 123. Yale University 1999)
"There is an uncomfortable feeling that, in spite of striving for general principles to ensure objectivity, we are in fact imposing our own prejudices just as surely, if not as blatantly, as if we were simply selecting the lines that fit one theory and ignoring others that do not. It is quite possible that we may be failing altogether to recognize signs of astronomical practice because we are 'selecting them out' at an early stage as a result of looking for the wrong things."

There is another possibility which could make matters much more difficult for the identification of foresights. Could it be, that instead of having the foresight at the extreme limit of visibility when viewed from the backsight, it was arranged so that it was just out of view? This idea may seem strange, but at Avebury, there is an arrangement which hints at this possibility. Caroline Malone, (*English Heritage Book of Avebury*. Batsford, 1989. Page 99) concerning Silbury Hill, states "*The mound is high, and yet it is not visible from within the Avebury circles*". This is not strictly true. The top of Silbury Hill can be glimpsed when standing a little to the west of the large concrete plinth which marks the position where the Obelisk once stood. However from the plinth itself the view of Silbury Hill is blocked by a huge stone, the central one of three in the perimeter of the southern inner circle. It seems strange that the view of Silbury Hill should be blocked when standing at such an important point as the Obelisk, the centre of the southern inner ring, and yet visible from a point a few yards to the west. It may be accidental, but it gives the distinct impression of being deliberate. Was this the basis for some occult rite, where the primary object was hidden from view, or occulted? If this were the case, then perhaps we should look for sightlines where the foresight is lost from view just before the observer reaches the backsight and it may help to explain why so many of Thom's sightlines could not be found.

This leaves any investigator with severe problems: namely how to identify a sightline when the foresight can not be seen from the backsight. This difficulty is not intractable if enough such sightlines can be identified. It may be possible to identify characteristics and properties of them, such as how close to the backsight the observer had to be before the foresight was obscured, or the direction and distance to the nearest point from which observations would be possible, or the length of time between making the last possible observation and the time when the Sun, or Moon, would have been seen behind the foresight, if it had been visible from the backsight. Strangely enough, for observations of the extreme rising or setting points of the Moon, it would not matter too much if the foresight could not be seen from the backsight, provided that the foresight was visible from points fairly close to the backsight. This is because the Moon would only be seen to rise or set with its extreme declination on very rare occasions and so this extreme position would have to be found by extrapolation as described by Thom. In this case the backsight would only act as a reference point.

Many people will regard the situation described above as extremely unlikely, but it is possible and we should keep open minds when setting criteria for sightlines. We do not know how Neolithic people thought, so it is vitally important not to ascribe our scientific methodology to them, or as Ruggles said we may *"select things out"* and lose valuable insights.

When Ruggles set out to check the validity of Thom's accurate Scottish alignments, he set objective criteria to try to prevent the subjective inclusion of sightlines. These criteria depended very much on the orientation of upright slabs and stone alignments, which tend to give rather low resolution directions, but he almost totally ignored the nature of the horizon indicated by these directions. Perhaps partly as a result he found virtually no evidence for high precision alignments and concluded that Thom had been wrong to class many of them as such. It is obvious though that the horizon is the vital element in this scenario. People watching the Sun set over the sea or distant hill, wait till the last glimmer of the sun disappears. I have seen dozens of people on a promenade, standing still watching the sunset and then continuing their walk as soon as the Sun vanished. Other people have watched the Sun set over hills. Some have climbed higher to try to see the Sun set for a second time. Others perhaps moved sideways to try to see the Sun in a gap between two hills and tried to see the last fleeting rays in the lowest part of the gap. This behavior is common and there is no reason to believe that our distant ancestors would not have behaved in a similar manner. In the last case, if they had marked the spot where they were standing, when they saw the last traces of the Sun, they would have made a solar observation with an accuracy of about one minute of arc, or one sixtieth of a degree. There is nothing fundamentally difficult about this procedure.

There was a very practical reason why a direction indicator was required for Moonrise observations at the time of the minor standstill. Human life was too short for an observer to witness more than two or three such events, as they were over eighteen years apart. It could have been even worse for many observers, as many people had short lives and it may have been a once in a lifetime experience and only then if visibility had been good. Extreme sunrise observations, weather permitting, could be done every year, but moonrise observations at the time of the standstills could only have been done for a few months every eighteen years and that would have made it desirable to have memory aids, or some form of help for new observers.

Because the declination of the Moon changes rapidly, it is very unlikely that the time of moonrise would correspond with the time of maximum or minimum declination and Thom realised that some form of extrapolation was needed. This required enough space to observe moonrises on the days both preceding and following maximum declination. At this site this space is provided for by the upper track, which is ideally placed and long enough for the purpose. Where the upper track overlooks the cutting, it appears to be built up to form a platform. The age of this platform is unknown, but if it could be shown to be contemporary with the ring, it would be strong evidence for the observatory theory.

NAMES

Pen Creigiau'r Llan means the top (or end or head) of the rocks of the Church (or possibly parish, or village), whilst Eglwys Gwyddelod can be translated as Irishman's Church. This is interesting as both refer to sacred places, but after an elapsed period of about four thousand years, the possibility of this correspondence of names being anything other than chance is very slim.

CONCLUSIONS

There is considerable evidence to support the view that Eglwys Gwyddelod and the immediate surroundings contain the remains of a solar and lunar observatory. The method of identifying the foresight was new to me, but similar methods seem to have been used in other areas. The method works extremely well and successfully indicates a foresight that would otherwise be missed.

I am of the opinion that much useful information remains to be discovered. Accurate theodolite surveys would be a check on my calculated declinations and also enable accurate horizon profiles to be constructed that would enable the point on the horizon where the rising Sun would first appear. If my results are confirmed then excavation of parts of both tracks, and in particular where the upper track is built up, could perhaps establish the dates when they were made.

The ring itself does not seem to be involved with any accurate observations as the rising points of the Sun and Moon are not visible from it. It seems fairly certain though that the ceremonies taking place within and around the ring would be intimately connected to the solar and lunar observations being made within a short distance of the ring.

DATA FOR THE SITE

Information obtained from O.S.maps.

Latitude	52.582 N
Grid correction	-1.568

Eglwys Gwyddelod platform

National grid East	SH 66.266
National Grid North	SH 0.193
Height	262 metres

Pen Creigiau'r Llan

National grid East	SN 74.528
National Grid North	SN 93.928
Height	507 metres

Calculated values

True bearing	125.605	
Distance	10.37km.	6.443miles

Declination non-lunar	-19.909
Declination lunar, mean parallax	-19.100

Pumlumon Summit Cairn

National grid East	78.975
National Grid North	86.950
Height	752 metres

Calculated values

True bearing	134.611	
Distance	18.355 km.	11.405miles
Declination non-lunar	-24.279	

The refraction correction was based on data provided by Thom. Anyone repeating the calculations may obtain slightly different results if the refraction data is different. The grid reference and heights were the best that could be obtained from the 1:25000 scale maps, but may be in error by small amounts.

CHAPTER 6

POSSIBLE REASONS FOR THE DESIGN OF
TYPE A AND TYPE B RINGS

After surveying several hundred stone rings, Alexander Thom found that a considerable number of them were not true circles, but circles that had been flattened on one side. These rings fell into two distinct groups, which he called Type A and Type B. Two or three of the flattened circles did not quite fit into these classes, but were very similar. These are Type D and type B_2. Below are surveys of two rings from Mid Wales that I made, one is a Type A ring and the other a Type B. These diagrams illustrate the geometries proposed by Thom.

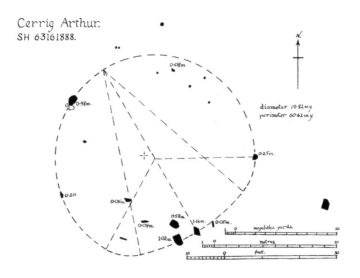

Type A ring

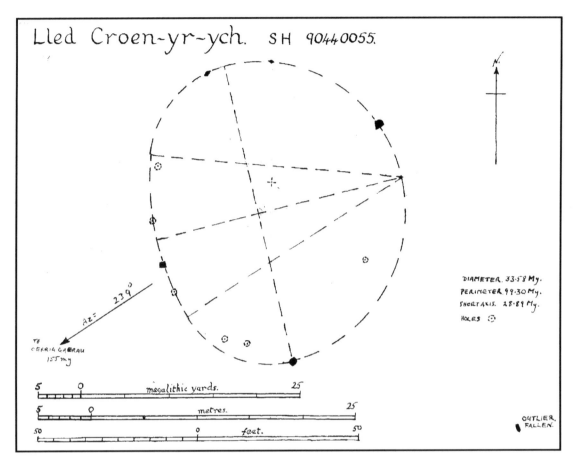

Type B ring

For rings with unit long axis the relative dimensions are shown below and the other two types are included.

Ring type	Long axis	Short axis	Perimeter
Type A	1.0000	0.9114	3.0591
Type B	1.0000	0.8604	2.9572
Type A$_2$ (Type D)	1.0000	0.9343	3.0840
Type B$_2$	1.0000	0.8091	2.8746
True circle	1.0000	★★★★★	3.1416

The short axis or perimeter of a given ring can be obtained by multiplying the length of the long axis of the ring by the corresponding factor in the above table.

In Type A rings a circle and three radii at 120 degree intervals are set out. The end of one radius acts as the centre for the long radius arc and the middle points of the other two radii act as centres for the short arcs. In Type B rings a diameter of a circle is divided into three equal lengths and these dividing points locate the centres of the short arcs. The end of a radius at right angles to this diameter acts as the centre for the long arc. Type D rings are similar to Type A rings, but the centres for the short arcs are one third of the way along the radii instead of half. Type B_2 rings are similar to Type B, but the centres of the short arcs are half way along the radii.

Two interesting relationships were found that related the dimensions of Type A and Type B rings to the perimeter of the basic circle, that is, a circle with a diameter equal to the long axis of the ring. These are given below.

Type A:

Perimeter	3.0591	Perimeter true circle	3.1416
Long axis	1.0000	Short axis	0.9114
Sum	**4.0591**	**Sum**	**4.0530**
Difference in sums	**0.0061**		

Type B:

Four times long axis	4.0000		
Less short axis	0.8604		
Difference	**3.1396**	**Perimeter basic circle**	**3.1416**
Difference in values	**0.0020**		

For Type D the same relationship holds as for Type A, but the accuracy is less. The error is **0.0081** compared with **0.0061** for Type A. The best that could be found for Type B_2 that was not too complex was:

2 x perimeter of ring – perimeter of circle = Long axis + 2 x short axis

The error here is **0.0106**, which is by far the largest error of the four types. Could this be the reason why only two Type D rings have been found and only one type B_2? Were the builders trying, in effect, to square the circle and incorporate their best solutions into these rings? Thom suggested that the rings were flattened in order to bring the perimeter closer to three times the diameter, but he did not seem to be totally convinced. The above figures seem to indicate that they were attempting to do something rather more advanced. If so they were more successful with the Type B construction, but in both Type A and Type B rings it would be difficult to detect the errors by direct measurement.

OUTLIERS TO TYPE A RINGS

At the moment I know of four Type A rings which have outliers, but there could well be more. The distances of these outliers from the ring centres vary considerably. Three are quite close in and one is far out. If they were intended to be astronomical sightlines, as is often claimed, putting them near the ring would reduce their accuracy, but does not necessarily preclude their use as such, especially if they were there to indicate a more distant foresight. Perhaps though there was another explanation for their positioning. There appears to be a set of relationships between the distance of the outlier from the centre of the ring and the dimensions of the ring. These relationships are:

$$D = P/4 + M + S$$
$$D = P/4 + M - S$$
$$D = P/4 - M + S$$

Where: D is the distance of the outlier from the centre of the ring.
              P is the perimeter of a perfect circle with diameter M
              M is the length of the major axis of the ring
              S is the length of the minor axis of the ring.

The essential dimensions of the rings are given below, followed by the formulae that give the distances (L) to the outliers.

	Long diameter	Short diameter	Outlier dist.
Cerrig Arthur (Hoyle)	53.91ft.	49.134ft.	46.89ft.
Black Marsh (Thom)	76.0ft.	69.266ft.	53.98ft.
Castle Rigg (Thom)	107.1ft.	97.61ft.	296ft.
Brat's Hill (Waterhouse)	104ft.	94.78ft.	88.91ft.

The dimensions of Brat's Hill are those given by Thom as Waterhouse only gave an average diameter for the ring. The distance to the outlier is that quoted by Waterhouse. (*The Stone Circles of Cumbria*. John Waterhouse 1985. Phillimore)

Cerrig Arthur
$$D = P/4 + M - S = 0.7854 \star 53.91 + 46.89 - 49.13 = 47.12\text{ft.}$$
Outlier distance 46.89ft.

Black Marsh
$$D = P/4 - M + S = 0.7854 \star 76 - 76 + 69.266 = 52.956\text{ft.}$$
Outlier distance 53.977ft.

Castle Rigg
$$D = P/4 + M + S = 0.7854 \star 107.1 + 107.1 + 97.61 = 288.83\text{ft.}$$
Outlier distance 296ft.

Brat's Hill
$$D = P/4 + M - S = 0.7854 \star 104 + 104 - 94.78 = 90.90\text{ft.}$$
Outlier distance 88.91ft.

It has been reported that the outlier to Castle Rigg has been moved by a local farmer. As there are plough marks in the stone, it seems probable that it was once buried in the field and as it got in the way it was dug up and moved to the edge of the field by the road, where it now stands. If the above relationship is correct it indicates that the stone was moved about seven feet further from the ring.

It is interesting that Cerrig Arthur and Brat's Hill both use the same formula. I had considered the possibility that each ring would use a different formula and that would have limited the number of type A rings with outliers to three, or possibly four if P/4 were to be negative, but if several rings can use the same formula, then the number of such rings could be very much greater and it is possible that several other such rings could exist and may yet be found.

OUTLIERS TO TYPE B RINGS

A similar type of relationship exists for these rings:

Distance to outlier = 2 x one diam +/- the other diam

	Long diam.	Short diam.	Outlier dist.
Lled Croen yr Ych (Hoyle)	91.338ft.	78.581ft.	103.659ft
Bar Brook (Thom)	47.40ft.	41.04ft.	135.30ft.
Long Meg (Thom)	359.55ft.	310.35ft.	261.68ft.

Lled Croen-yr-ych.
2 x long diam. – short diam. = 2 ∗ 91.34ft – 78.58 = 104.10ft.
Outlier distance   103.66ft.

Bar brook
2 x long diam. + short diam. = 94.90 + 41.04 = 135.94ft.
Outlier distance   135.30ft.

Long Meg
2 x short diam. – long diam. = 620.70 – 359.55 = 261.15ft.
Outlier distance   261.68ft.

It would seem that another combination is possible ie.

2 x short diam. + long diam.

The relationships for Type B rings are particularly accurate and apart from the outlier at Castle Rigg, all the calculated results for Type A rings are within two feet of those measured on the ground. It is certain that other Type A and Type B rings with outliers exist, or existed, and it would be of great interest to determine if the distances of the outliers fit into the above patterns.

OUTLIERS TO TYPE D RINGS

I am aware of only one other flattened circle that has an outlier and that is Gray Croft near Seascale, which is a Type D ring.

The dimensions given by Waterhouse are:

Major axis = 27.2m; Minor axis = 24.4m; Distance to outlier 34m.
The sum of these is: 85.6m
The perimeter of a circle with diameter 27.2m is: 85.45m

It is one thing to tease out numerical relationships from the measured dimensions of megalithic rings, but it is quite a different matter to understand the reasons for them. These rings cover a region from Cumbria in the north, Derbyshire in the south and Mid Wales in the west, and perhaps even further afield, so it would seem these designs depend on more than the doodlings of one or two mathematically inquisitive individuals. In addition these rings appear to have been built over a long period of time, the large ones probably being considerably older than the smaller ones, which suggests that these ideas persisted.

If these relationships are valid, it indicates that the builders were fascinated with the perimeters of circles and wished to incorporate their discoveries within their rings. It must have been of great importance to them, but it does not give an answer to the question of why they went to such lengths. To a casual observer it is not at all apparent that flattened circles are not truly circular and the difference between the various types can only be determined by careful measurement. It is tempting to think that these designs, and built in relationships, conferred some special, perhaps magical, properties on the rings. It is possible that these flattened circles and their links to true circles were believed to form a bridge between this imperfect world and the realm of the perfect Gods. We will probably never understand the true nature of their beliefs. The problem is similar to that of understanding Christianity from the decrepit remains of old abandoned churches and their associated burial grounds. These built in mathematical relationships give no more than a hint of the richness and variety of their concepts and beliefs, but it is one of the few ways by which we can get a glimpse of their thought processes.

If these relationships are what they seem, it implies that some central body controlled the building of these rings and it raises more questions than it answers. Are there more Type A and B rings with outliers and if so do they have the same distance relationships? It seems that I was fortunate in surveying rings in Mid Wales as these included examples of almost all types of ring described by Thom and of particular importance here, a Type A ring and a Type B ring, both with outliers

CHAPTER 7

PRECIOUS STONES: SOURCES OF STONES FOR RING BUILDING

With the exception of Stonehenge and a handful of other rings, perhaps too little attention has been paid to the sources of the stones for building rings. It tends to be assumed that there were sufficient stones around, or within a few miles of the site, to satisfy the requirements of the ring builders. In some areas this was undoubtedly true. In other areas the available stones would quite quickly have been exhausted, especially the large ones with the shapes needed for upright monoliths, or for the kerbs of cairns, the sides and tops of cists and other specialised purposes. The search for suitable stones would then have to be widened and the work of transportation would have become much greater. Eventually, if the scale of the work warranted, it would have been necessary to quarry the stones, perhaps at considerable distance and the costs in time and labour would then have become enormous. This task is hard enough using metal tools, but before the Bronze Age, there were only tools of stone, wood, bone and antlers, so the quarrying of a suitably shaped stone weighing perhaps several tons, could have taken a small team of men weeks of toil and sweat. Even today large stones are expensive, but in the Neolithic period, their value must have been astronomical. The use of such stones in rings and cairns was justified only because of the utmost importance that these monuments had for the local society.

Crude though some circles look to us today, they must have been designed with care and considering the amount of work involved, every stone would have been regarded as essential to the monument as a whole. The construction must also have been done with great skill, as after four or five thousand years, many stones, both big and small, are still standing firmly and that is no mean achievement. If some of the stones had to be quarried, then "orders" for them would have had to be made to the quarry, or quarries, in advance, to avoid delays in construction. In large projects, there must have been some form of record keeping, otherwise there would have been chaos, mistakes would be made and perhaps some stones may not be made, whilst others could be duplicated. In work that perhaps lasted a few years, it would have been easy to forget exactly who made what, and human nature being what it is, some workers could have claimed for work that they had not done! This raises the question of how the work was organised. If the whole of society worked together co-operatively as a single team, then perhaps some of these problems could have been avoided, but they would then, as a group, have had to be single minded enough to complete such projects and this would have been made more difficult by having to break off to tend their animals, grow their crops, prepare food and perform the thousand and one jobs necessary for life. Small projects could have been done in this way, but the larger the project the less likely this method would have succeeded. To drive a large project through to completion must have required a small group of people with vision, planning ability and the necessary power and authority to organise sections of the local population into work groups and to maintain that organisation over prolonged periods. The extreme examples of such projects are Avebury and Silbury Hill, which must have taken several generations to complete. There is evidence that the bluestones at Stonehenge were transported manually from the Prescelly Hills in Pembrokeshire. If this is correct, it represents an extreme example of their organisational ability and the value given to certain stones.

The Kilmartin area in Western Scotland is famous for its standing stones, circles and large cairns. The building projects here were organised on a grand scale. It seems likely that the builders would have used the local stones very quickly and then would have had to widen their search. It was whilst looking at the cup and ring markings on the stones at Cairnbaan that I realised that the upper set of cup and ring marks was in a depressed area that looked quite like an old quarry and that the wet patch just below the cup and ring bearing rock was perhaps where some of the stones had been removed. Could it be that the cup and ring marks were old records of the stones quarried from this spot?

To a quarryman, making marks in the rock to record the completion of a piece of work, perhaps overseen by a supervisor, would be quite natural. The different marks could indicate the different sizes and shapes of stone produced. A single cup could perhaps represent a stone of the smallest size that was worth recording. A cup and single ring could represent a stone that was somewhat larger and the more rings, the larger the stone that had been produced. This would be consistent with the fact that single cups are the most abundant, whilst cups with many rings are much less common. A line from the centre of a cup and ring could perhaps indicate a stone that would be suitable for a tall upright. If there is any truth in this idea, then cup and ring marks would be likely to be found where there had been quarrying. Good stone that is easy to get at, often occurs in outcrops at the edges of hills and this is where many cup and ring marks are found. This would imply that the cup and ring carvings were made there, not because the position had a good view, but because the stone in such positions was, and still is, of good quality and was relatively easy to quarry and extract.

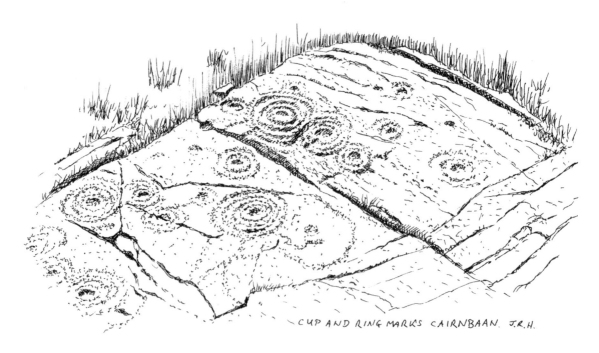

CUP AND RING MARKS CAIRNBAAN. J.R.H.

Cup and ring marks are usually included in the term rock art, but it is difficult to see the artistic value of a few depressions scattered over the face of a rock slab and most of the rock markings tend to be simple depressions, either singly or surrounded by a ring. If rock markings were broadly of two classes, true rock art and recording marks, it may help to explain why some slabs with markings on them have been used in megalithic tombs. After a large project had been completed, the recording marks would cease to have value and as they were often displayed on good and valuable slabs of rock, it would be natural to quarry them and use them in subsequent projects, in a way that would not show the marks, that is with the marks underneath, as is occasionally seen. This would also account for the weathering that has been observed around the marks on several such rocks, as a considerable period may have elapsed between one building project and the next.

One argument against this idea is that there are places where cup and ring marks are common, but there do not seem to be any corresponding stone circles or other megalithic structures which could have used the stones indicated by the marks. An example of such a place is Ilkley Moor. However this is a place where extensive building took place during the industrial revolution. Whole towns grew up creating a massive demand for stone and it is probable that any megalithic structures would have been plundered. In my home town of Haslingden my father always referred to a particular hill as Thirteen Stones Hill. On old O.S. maps the name appears some distance north west of the highest point, with a grid reference close to SD 763 344. It is not easy to be more exact as the maps used during the Second World War used a different grid system. On more modern maps the hill is called Haslingden Moor. I have walked over that hill many times but have seen no trace of any stones. If there ever was a stone circle there, it may still be possible to find traces of the stone sockets. Not far away there are quarries and I suspect that quarrymen, or builders, regarded the stones as too valuable to leave there. It may be that records describing the stones exist, but if so I have no knowledge of them. If no stones ever existed there, it seems strange that the hill ever had such a name. Recently I have been made aware of new evidence concerning this name and it is described in chapter ten.

It may be possible to obtain evidence for, or against, this idea by correlating the number and size of megalithic stones used in an area, such as Kilmartin, which is relatively undisturbed, with the number and type of cup and ring marks on surrounding rocks. The process would be difficult and time consuming and with no guarantee of success, but may produce worthwhile results.

It is clear that not all rock carvings are records. There are lots of highly decorative carvings which clearly have other purposes. Many of the stones in the Irish passage tombs, such as Newgrange and Knowth are richly decorated with spirals, zig zags and more complex patterns and similar carvings are to be found on Anglesey at Barclodiad y Gawres. Carvings of Axes are occasionally to be found on stones, such as those at Stonehenge. It is likely that the markings to be found on rocks were made for a variety of reasons, decorative, religious, representational, record keeping or just plain doodling.

CHAPTER 8

AN ALTERNATIVE TO THOM'S DESIGN
OF AVEBURY

Of all the Stone circles in the British Isles, the great ring at Avebury is by far and away the largest and it is so great that the remains of two other very large circles are to be found enclosed within it. The stones of this huge ring are on an equally massive scale. Surrounding it is a huge ditch between 23 and 33 feet deep, 70 feet wide at the top and about 13 feet wide at the bottom. Excavations have revealed that this ditch was carefully made, having very steeply sloping sides and a flat bottom. Estimates for the time taken to construct this complex vary, but it must have taken hundreds of workers many years to complete it. In addition these workers would have had to be housed, clothed, fed and supplied with tools. The supply of leather for ropes would have necessitated the slaughter of very large numbers of cattle, which would in turn have provided the shoulder blades that were used for shovels and then large numbers of deer antlers would have been needed for picks. Baskets would be needed for moving the earth and all these would have had to be worked with flint tools. The organisation involved would have been phenomenal. If only local people had worked on it at times when they were not farming, then the time taken to finish the project would have been several times longer.

The shape of this ring is unusual in that the perimeter consists of arcs which meet at "corners". This has given rise to the idea that the first stage of construction was the rough marking out of the line of the ditch, which was then excavated by gangs of workers. Each gang, it has been suggested, was given a separate section of the ditch to excavate. The line of each section was then determined by the gang working on it and these sections then joined up in a rather haphazard manner. The arcs of stones were then set out at some distance from the inside edge of the ditch. Caroline Malone has expressed this idea as follows "*No amount of clever geometry or astro-archaeological theorising can really pretend that the Neolithic builders had sophisticated survey equipment at their disposal. The great monument has all the appearance of having been paced out roughly on the ground. After that, teams of workers excavated the ditch, probably starting at different points, and meeting, somewhat haphazardly, on the way.*" (Caroline Malone. *English Heritage Book of Avebury*. Batsford 1989. Page 105). Burl also thought that the ditch was dug before the stones were erected and that these stones followed a line about ten metres inside the edge of the ditch. (*Aubrey Burl. Prehistoric Avebury. Yale University 1979. Page 181.*)

THE GREAT STONES OF AVEBURY. J.R.H.

It is difficult to believe that this huge undertaking, with all the associated planning, was to make a ring of stones, whose shape was going to be determined by the whims of gangs of diggers. Is it reasonable to believe that the shape of this ring, the ring that required so much determined effort and organisation and that took generations to complete, would not be exactly determined in advance of the construction? Would the instigators of this colossal project commit themselves to this huge undertaking without knowing exactly what they were about to make? One can only assume that this ring was designed in advance with the utmost care. The shape of it must have been that intended by the designers and the "corners" must have been intentional. Nothing else makes any sense.

Thom has shown that rings throughout the British Isles have been set out with great care and conform to particular geometries, such as circles, flattened circles, ellipses, egg shaped rings and a few compound rings. Why then should Avebury be any different? Is it reasonable to believe that the largest and most imposing stone circle in Britain would not have a design that reflected its massive nature? Setting out the design on the ground would undoubtedly have presented great problems, but in spite of having no sophisticated survey equipment at their disposal, the site surveyors used what simple tools they had with great skill and, as is shown by Thom's meticulous survey, set out the arcs with great accuracy. The question is not "Was the ring set out to a preconceived design?", but "What was the preconceived design?"

Thom attempted to answer this question and produced a design that fitted the known parts of the ring extremely well. The problem that many people have with this design is that it does not have much in common with the design of other compound or egg shaped rings, in that only one Pythagorean triangle was used and that was used in an asymmetrical manner. In addition there seems to be little justification for choosing the positions of some of the centres of the arcs or of their radii, other than they were multiples of five or ten Megalithic Yards. It is easy to criticize, but is it possible to produce a design that is more in line with the layout of other types of ring and still fits the stones as well? Answering that question is the task that I set myself.

In trying to elucidate the design, it is necessary to make assumptions. Clearly the first assumption is that the ring was carefully designed and that it is possible to recover this design. As the remains are far from complete, it is necessary to make use of some guiding principles. Thom assumed that the design used a single 3, 4, 5 Pythagorean triangle and that the essential lengths were multiples of five Megalithic Yards. The two longest arcs were then assumed to have the same radius of 750 Megalithic Yards.

The assumptions used in my construction are firstly that the design was basically symmetrical about an axis that ran from around west north-west to east south-east. Secondly that it used Pythagorean triangles in a similar way to the use of them in egg type rings, but in a more complex manner in that a large number of such triangles were used and that these triangles were not only interrelated, but interlocked. Thirdly it assumes that the unit used was not the Megalithic Yard but the old foot, occasionally used singly, but more often in groups of three and from time to time in groups of five. The values of the old foot and the old yard which best fits the stones were found to be 0.986 ft. and 2.958 feet respectively. There is a sort of logic to this design and when the perimeter was calculated, it was found to be related to the dimensions of four of the triangles used.

The design is illustrated in the following four diagrams. All dimensions are in Old Yards.

Geometry of Avebury 1

To fit the stones

1. Rotate the design 19.33 degrees clockwise
   about point D

2. Move point D to position
   X=605.44 and Y=592.23
   in Thom's co-ordinate system.

3. Adjust the scale so that
   one old yard equals 2.958 ft.

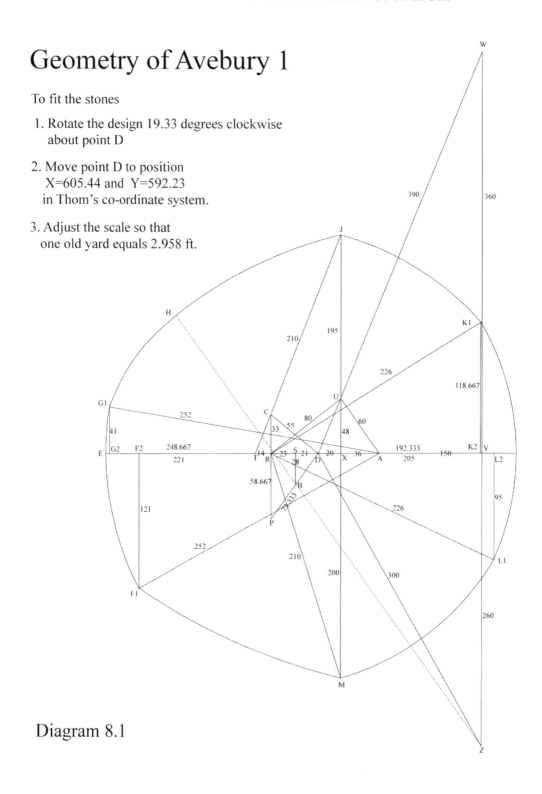

Diagram 8.1

Geometry of Avebury 2
Arc Centres

P is the centre of arc J K1
R is the centre of arc K1 L1
C is the centre of arc L1 M
W is the centre of arc M F1
A is the centre of arc F1 G1
B is the centre of arc G1 H
Z is the centre of arc H J

H is on ZB produced so
that ZH equals ZJ

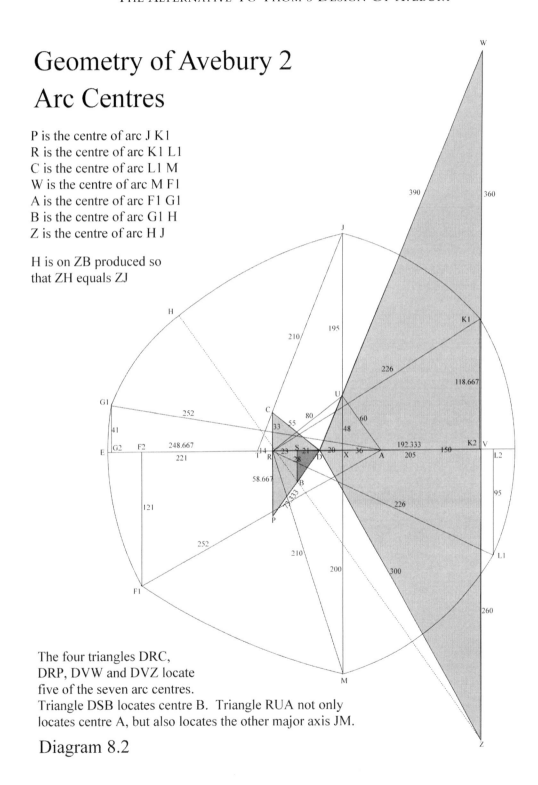

The four triangles DRC,
DRP, DVW and DVZ locate
five of the seven arc centres.
Triangle DSB locates centre B. Triangle RUA not only
locates centre A, but also locates the other major axis JM.

Diagram 8.2

Geometry of Avebury 3
Ends of arcs

These three pairs of triangles locate
all the six corners of the ring. These
are J, K1, L1, M, F1,and G1.
H is not situated at a corner, but
where two arcs merge. H is on ZB
produced and ZH equals ZJ.

In each pair of triangles, the
hypotenuse of one equals the
hypotenuse of the other.

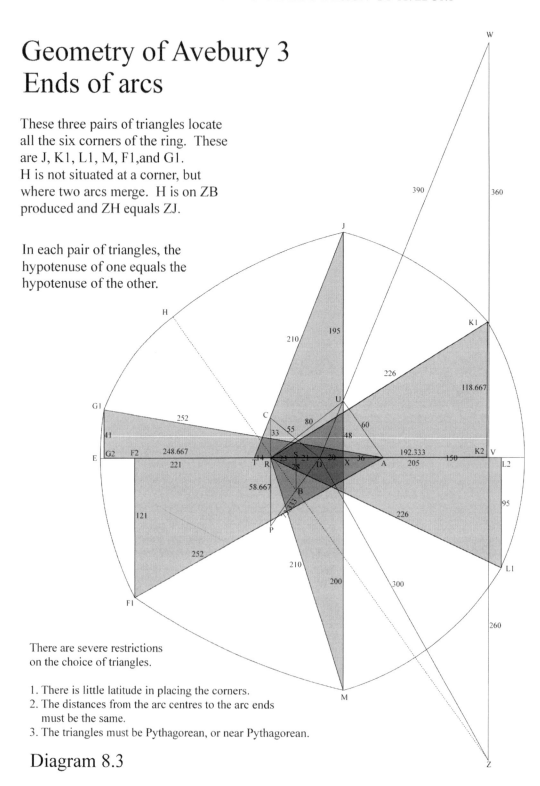

There are severe restrictions
on the choice of triangles.

1. There is little latitude in placing the corners.
2. The distances from the arc centres to the arc ends
   must be the same.
3. The triangles must be Pythagorean, or near Pythagorean.

Diagram 8.3

Geometry of Avebury 4

Long Radius Arcs and Arc Centre B

This illustrates the two flat arcs HJ and
MF1 with centres Z and W.
It also shows the arc with centre B which
merges at H with arc HJ.

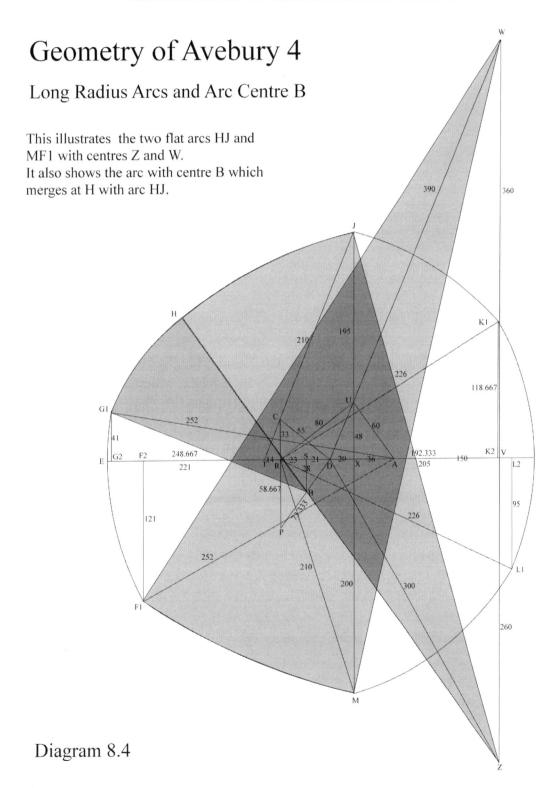

Diagram 8.4

The finalised design is illustrated in diagram 8.1. The apparent complexity of it hides the symmetry and simplicity of the concepts inherent in this plan. Diagram 8.2 shows the seven arc centres P, R, C, W, A, B and Z. Five of them P, R, C, W and Z are directly located by four Pythagorean, or near Pythagorean triangles.

$$P \text{ is the centre for arc } JK_1$$
$$R \text{ is the centre for arc } K_1L_1$$
$$C \text{ is the centre for arc } L_1M$$
$$W \text{ is the centre for arc } MF_1$$
$$A \text{ is the centre for arc } F_1G_1$$
$$B \text{ is the centre for arc } G_1H$$
$$Z \text{ is the centre for arc } HJ$$

Centre A is 100 old yards from R and is connected by triangle RUA to the other triangles and this triangle also locates the other axis of the ring JM. Centre B is located by the perfect Pythagorean triangle DSB with sides of 21, 28 and 35 old yards. The triangles DRC, DRP, DCP, RUX, AUX, and RUA are all based on 3, 4, 5 Pythagorean triangles. Triangles DWV and DUX are exact multiples of 5,12,13 Pythagorean triangles. Triangle DZV is a ten fold size 15, 26, 30 near Pythagorean triangle which is an excellent approximation for a right angled triangle in which the hypotenuse is twice the length of the short side. Point H is on ZB produced and ZH equals ZJ. BH is very closely equal to BG_1.

Diagram 8.3 shows the three pairs of near Pythagorean triangles which locate the six "corners" of the ring. In each pair the hypotenuse of one equals the hypotenuse of the other. The design requires that RK_1 equals RL_1 and that AG_1 equals AF_1, but not that TJ should equal MR. The point T seems to play no essential part in the design and it would appear that it is there merely to form a triangle with a hypotenuse of 210 and so pair up with triangle RXM. There is a perfect Pythagorean triangle EXJ (not highlighted), with sides 195, 216 and 291, which links the left hand side of the main axis with the point J. This triangle could have been used to ensure that the two main axes were exactly perpendicular to each other.

Diagram 8.4 shows the two flat arcs with their corresponding radii and also the arc G_1H, which runs into arc HJ without forming a "corner". The other arcs are not shown shaded in as it would confuse the diagram too much, but it is quite easy to see where they are. In all cases the radii joining the ends of the arcs to the arc centre are very similar in length.

Any change to the length of any side in any triangle not only changes one or more sides of that triangle, but also the distances of that point from other points, so that lengths which should be equal, will no longer be so. For example, if point W were to be moved closer to V then not only would the distances WD and WV change, but the distances WM and WF_1 would also change and they would no longer be equal. This would necessitate a repositioning of M or F_1, or perhaps both, and this would have a knock on effect on other points. In addition the triangles must be Pythagorean, or near Pythagorean and this places further very considerable restrictions on the design.

Thom listed the deviations of the stones from his arcs and added together the squares of these deviations, in order to determine how well the plan fitted the existing stones. This came to 192.88, but would have been closer to 220 if he had considered stone 98 to be on the perimeter of the ring instead of on his basic circle. The sum of the squares of the deviations in this construction, without having to make special provision for stone 98, is 172.81. This is 20 smaller than for Thom's construction and therefore this plan fits the stones rather better. Although the arcs are similar in both proposed plans, in my plan arc centre A is little shorter, and arc centre B a little longer, than in Thom's design and as a result stone 39 is included in arc centre B, instead of arc centre A and this produces a more natural and better fit.

It was only when I had determined the perimeter of the ring that I discovered a property that may give some clue as to the purpose of the design. The perimeter of the ring is 1195.206 old yards. As can be seen from diagram 8.2 the sum of the five lengths defining the two large triangles DVW and DVZ is 1460 old yards (the common side DV is only counted once) and the corresponding sum for the two equivalent triangles DRC and DRP is 264 old yards. The difference between these two is 1196, which is well within an old yard of the length of the perimeter. This could be a coincidence, but as the difference is only about one part in 1500 it is unlikely to be so. If it were intentional, then it would explain why the centres of the two flat arcs are so far away and account for the peculiar shape of this ring. It would imply that the builders were endeavoring to try to "square the circle", that is, to try to find an exact correspondence between the lengths of straight lines and lengths of arcs of circles. If that is so, they had a remarkably good attempt at doing something that we now know to be impossible. In view of similar types of relationships in the design of flattened circles, it would not seem to be unreasonable to assume that this was one of the guiding principles in the design of Avebury.

Setting out this plan on the ground would have been much easier than setting out Thom's design, as once the two main axes had been accurately marked out, all other points could have been measured from these and the position of corner points could have been cross checked by measuring the hypotenuse of each triangle. Setting out of the arcs would not have been as difficult as has sometimes been suggested. Provided that the sagitta, that is, the distance between the middle point of the arc and its chord, is known, all other parts of the arc could be determined without any further reference to the centre of the arc. A possible method for doing this has been discussed in the chapter on Megalithic mathematics. Thom described another method which is outlined below. The principle is shown in diagram 8.5.

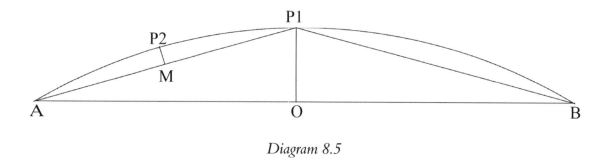

Diagram 8.5

OP_1 is the sagitta of arc AP_1B and MP_2 is the sagitta of arc AP_2P_1.

If it is required to construct an arc between points A and B, it is first necessary to find the position P_1 of the mid point of the arc. This may have been done by measuring from the central point of the circle, but it is more likely that it was done by calculation of the length of the sagitta. A second point P_2 is found by finding the mid point M of AP_1 and making MP_2 equal to one quarter of OP_1. A point on the arc half way between A and P_2 could be determined by finding the mid point of chord AP_2 and moving outwards a distance one quarter of MP_2. In this way as many points can be found as are required. This method, unlike the method previously described, does not produce absolutely accurate solutions, but it is far easier to apply and the accuracy improves as the arcs become flatter. The arc with the greatest inaccuracy when constructed by this method is arc centre A. This has a radius of 226 old yards and a subtended angle of 56.22 degrees. The correct value for distance MP_2 is 6.765 old yards. The distance calculated by the above method is 6.664old yards. The error is only 0.1 old yards, but by splitting the arc into two portions and treating these separately, the error would be reduced to a small fraction of this. Any errors introduced by this method would be small compared with the errors in setting up the stones in their sockets.

If the designers were aware of the theorem of Pythagoras, or of the theorem concerning the products of the portions of intersecting chords, then the sagitta of an arc could have been found accurately by calculation.

Using the calculation methods described, it would not then even be necessary to locate the centres W and Z on the ground and the often quoted difficulties of measuring from these points would have been completely removed. We can not know if they were aware of these methods, but considering their interest in right angled triangles and geometry in general, it seems possible that a few gifted individuals may have learned how to do it.

In building the ring, it tends to be assumed that the ditch was dug before the stones were brought to the site and therefore the shape of the ditch determined the shape of the ring. The evidence for this comes from packing stones which originally came from the bottom of the ditch and are now found around the bases of some of the standing stones. It follows from this that the ditch was dug before some of the stones were erected. It is possible though that the stones were brought to the site and left close to their intended positions before the ditch was dug and the erection of them left for the final stage of construction. Ordering the work in this way would have advantages. By gathering the stones first, the local population would have committed themselves to the project and could get some idea of what the final result would be like. This would help them to persevere with the gruelling toil of digging the ditch. When this was completed the erection of the stones would have proceeded relatively quickly and the grand opening would have followed. Digging the ditch after the stones had been erected would have been very discouraging and disheartening and would have entailed extra work constantly clearing the site.

This order of events is hinted at by the ring at Arbor Low in Derbyshire. Here a ring of stones is surrounded by a ditch, but the stones, with one exception, are all lying flat and the exception is only raised at a small angle. No stone hole sockets have ever been discovered, so it is likely, though by no means certain, that the stones have never been erected. The ditch has been dug through solid limestone and blocks of over a ton have been removed and placed in the surrounding bank, but none of this stone has been selected for use in the ring. All the stones inside the ditch have come from an outcrop at some distance. This suggests that the stones inside the ditch were selected and placed there before the ditch was made, otherwise it is likely that stones from the ditch would have been used. Erection of the stones was to be the last task of the ring builders, but for some reason was never completed. The same order of construction could have been followed at Avebury.

J.R.H.   THE PROSTRATE STONES OF ARBOR LOW.

Thom proposed a remarkable design for Avebury. It fitted the stones extremely well and defined a value for the Megalithic Yard that was consistent with his other derivations for the unit. This design presented here is, I believe, more convincing. Both can not be correct and perhaps neither is. There are several reasons though why this construction is more probable.

1. It fits the stones more accurately than Thom's design.
2. The geometry has more in common with other egg type rings.
3. It accounts for the near symmetry of the ring.
4. It accounts for the unusual shape of the ring and its corners.
5. It explains why two of the arc centres are so far outside the ring.
6. The perimeter is related to the dimensions of the four triangles that locate most arc centres.
7. All distances and positions are governed by the requirements of Pythagorean triangles which are so interlocked that there is a certain amount of inevitability about the design.

Pythagorean triangles are not uncommon, in fact an infinite number exist and close approximations to Pythagorean triangles are even more common. It is rare though to find such triangles having the correct sizes to satisfy the necessary conditions. For example the points F_1 and G_1 are located at two of the corners on the left. AF_1 and AG_1 must both be equal and be close to 252. The short sides in each must be close to 121 and 41 in order to be in the correct places for the corners. Two different Pythagorean triangles must then be found having these lengths. Estimating the probability of this happening by chance is a difficult problem, but the likelihood of it must be quite low. The fact that it does happen and for all points on the ring, seems to indicate that that is indeed how the ring was designed.

If this design is correct it would be possible to locate important points to within a few feet and as the builders must have marked these in some way, it may be possible to find evidence for them. If there were holes in these positions, perhaps not unlike the Aubrey holes at Stonehenge, then it should not be too difficult to find them. Again if there were holes in the chalk that were later filled in with other materials then ground penetrating radar may be of some use in detecting them. At least in principle, it should be possible to determine if this design is correct. The problem here though is that almost all the arc centres are under houses, gardens or other structures and many have probably been destroyed. Only centre C and possibly centre P are accessible and the latter appears to be very close to, or even under, the side of the A45.

THE AVENUE AND SANCTUARY

Thom surveyed and published the plans of the West Kennet Avenue (A. Thom and A.S. Thom. *Megalithic Remains in Britain and Brittany*, page 44). From these it is possible to determine the distances between the stones to an accuracy of two feet, or better (1mm on the plan is equivalent to 6.787 feet on the ground). The average distance between opposite pairs of stones was found to be very close to 47.36ft, which is 16 old yards and the average distance between stones in the same row was very close to 78.62ft, which is effectively 16 of the old five foot units. What is clear is that the ratio of the width of the avenue to the distance between adjacent stones in the same row is in the ratio of 3 to 5 and both distances relate to the length of the old foot. It is difficult to avoid the conclusion that the old yard and foot were used in setting out the West Kennet Avenue.

Burl (Burl, *Stone Circles of the British Isles*, page 318) lists the diameters of the various rings in the Sanctuary at the end of the West Kennet Avenue. Using these data it was not found possible to find any unit that fitted all, or even most, of these diameters and it must be concluded that either no single unit was used or that the intended diameters of the rings were not recovered with sufficient accuracy.

ESSENTIAL DATA FOR THE CONSTRUCTION.

Lengths in feet for this section.

Best unit	2.958 feet
Rotation angle	19.33 degrees clockwise
Sum of squares of displacements of stones from perimeter	172.810
Sum of displacements	0.735
RMS	2.0785

Coordinates of essential points in Thom's coordinate system

Centre	X	Y
D	605.44	592.23
C	514.94	727.42
W	1,376.61	1,450.21
A	761.75	537.40
B	519.41	534.64
P	425.18	471.56
R	482.63	635.31
Z	769.56	-280.36

Triangle sizes in old yards.

Triangle	Short side	Medium side	Hypotenuse	Comment
RUA	60	80	100	Locates arc centres A and R. Also locates the other axis.
RUX	48	64	80	
AUX	36	48	60	
RCD	22	44	55	Locates centre C
RPD	44	58.6666	73.3333	Locates centre P
SBD	21	28	35	Locates centre B

All the above are perfect 3,4,5 triangles.

Large triangles

DWV	150	360	390	

Perfect 5, 12, 13 triangle

DZV	150	260	300	

10 times 15, 26, 30.017 triangle. Near perfect.

Corner locating triangles.

TJX	78	195	210.021	Near perfect
RMX	64	200	210.990	Near perfect
RK1K2	118.6666	192.3333	225.995	Near perfect
RL1L2	95	205	225.942	Near perfect
AG1G2	41	248.6666	252.024	Near perfect
AF1F2	121	221	251.956	Near perfect

Radii of arcs in Old Yards.

PJ	261.616	(156.969 Five Foot Units)
PK1	261.609	(156.965 Five Foot Units)
Nominal Value	261.6666	(157.000 Five Foot Units)
RK1	225.995	
RL1	225.942	
Nominal Value	226	
CL1	241.680	(145.007 Five Foot Units)
CM2	41.640	(144.978 Five Foot Units)
Nominal value	241.6666	(145.000 Five Foot Units)
WM	574.891	
WF1	574.966	
Nominal Value	575	
AF1	251.956	
AG1	252.024	
Nominal Value	252	
ZJ	473.207	
ZH = ZJ =	473.207	
Nominal Value	473.3333	(284.000 Five Foot Units)
ZB	288.210	
Assumed to be 288.3333	(173. 000 Five Foot Units)	

BH = ZH - ZB   184.997

BG1   185.015

Nominal Value   185

The largest error is less than 0.12 old yards, which is about four inches or 10 centimetres and most are very much smaller than this.

For calculating the errors in stone positions, the nominal values of the radii were used. Coordinates of stones and distances from perimeter. (1 o.y. = 2.958 ft.)

Stone	X	Y	Distance from centre	Error
Arc C	ft.	ft.	ft.	ft.
1	733.7	44.0	717.58	2.73
3	659.7	28.0	714.25	-0.60
4	624.2	19.3	716.50	1.65
5	588.4	13.9	717.30	2.45
6	551.6	12.3	716.06	1.21
7	515.1	9.5	717.92	3.07
8	478.0	16.6	711.78	-3.07
98	769.9	64.9	709.89	-4.96
Arc W				
9	445.3	23.4	1,703.86	3.01
10	413.8	46.2	1,702.43	1.58
11	377.9	74.1	1,700.33	-0.52
12	357.1	94.1	1,696.60	-4.25
13	327.7	112.4	1,699.99	-0.86
14	300.6	136.2	1,698.36	-2.49
15	272.0	158.8	1,699.39	-1.46

16	243.5	183.0	1,699.93	-0.92
17	216.3	205.0	1,702.02	1.17
18	188.9	229.8	1,702.96	2.11
19	163.5	255.5	1,702.64	1.79
20	140.0	285.0	1,699.10	-1.75
21	120.6	305.7	1,699.26	-1.59
22	103.1	323.1	1,700.65	-0.2
23	85.0	344.0	1,700.58	-0.27
24	61.8	371.3	1,700.82	-0.03

Arc A

30	19.3	624.4	747.53	2.11
31	24.9	663.0	747.48	2.06
32	33.3	698.3	746.01	0.59
33	43.7	731.3	743.77	-1.65
34	55.5	764.4	741.84	-3.58
35	62.9	790.1	743.14	-2.28
36	69.2	815.0	746.12	0.70
37	85.0	849.8	745.38	-0.04
38	98.5	884.6	748.63	3.22

Arc B

39	123.6	910.5	545.84	-1.39
40	146.8	936.9	548.32	1.09
41	175.2	962.4	549.06	1.83
42	206.7	984.7	548.04	0.81
43	237.6	1,002.9	546.52	-0.71
44	270.3	1,022.5	547.78	0.55

45	292.5	1,031.2	545.95	-1.28
46	315.8	1,042.0	546.69	-0.54

Arc Z

50	461.1	1,085.4	1,400.16	0.04

Arc P

68	1,033.4	946.2	771.50	-2.51

Arc lengths in old yards. (Three of the radii are integer in old feet and old five foot units)

Arc	Centre	Radius	Chord length	Sagitta	Arc length
J – K1	P	261.6667	149.319	10.877	151.423
K1 – L1	R	226	214.042	26.946	222.976
L1 – M	C	241.6667	175.801	16.553	179.928
M – F1	W	575	201.162	8.865	202.202
F1 – G1	A	252	164.346	13.774	167.407
G1 – H	B	185	101.213	7.056	102.519
H – J	Z	473.3333	167.859	7.500	168.751

Total perimeter length is **1195.206**

Perimeter of triangles DWV and DZV less common side is 1460
Perimeter of triangles DCR and DPR less common side is 264
Difference= **1196**

CHAPTER 9

OTHER SITES

THE WAUN OER ALIGNMENT

This group of stones lies on a plateau between the end of the Cadair Idris range and the sea. It is close to a very narrow road that climbs steeply from the village of Llwyngwril and is one of the few alignments in Mid Wales. The situation is very fine, with extensive views out to sea and to the Lleyn Peninsula in the north west.

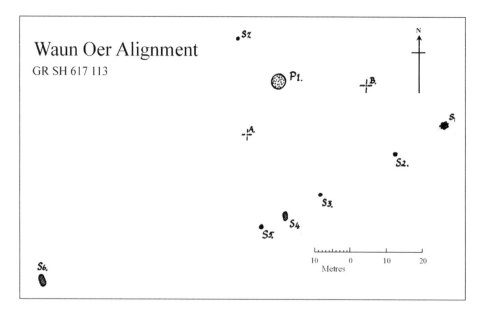

There are four stones still standing, S2, S3, S5 and S7, though the last stone is not part of the alignment. Stone S1 lies flat amidst a pile of other stones. There are other piles of stones around and they may be due to field clearances. Stone S4 is interesting as, though fallen, it has a cup and ring mark on it. Stone S6 lies flat and is not in direct line with the other stones. Points A and B are the positions from which the site was triangulated. In addition, the distances between most of the stones, were measured directly, which was of particular importance for S6.

As there is higher land to the north east, the alignment can only be used as a sightline in a south westerly direction where there is only sea. The tops of stones S2 and S3 line up accurately with the horizon and they indicate an azimuth of 242.5 degrees. The declination is about -17.2 degrees which corresponds to the lower limb of the Sun at Candlemas or Martinmas. It is likely then that this alignment determines calendar dates one eighth of a year before and after the Winter Solstice.

Waun Oer Alignment looking south west and showing the fallen stone S1.

Looking over stone S2 towards S3, with the sea beyond. Note that the tops of these stones appear to indicate the sea horizon.

BRYN-Y-CASTELL. G.R. SH 6151 0161

Bryn-y-castell is a farm about a mile to the south of Bryncrug, near Tywyn and a short distance above the farm, there is a motte or mound. The top of this mound is about 15 metres in diameter and on the south east side there is a ditch cut into the solid rock. This separates the mound from a short level area, after which the slope again continues upwards. The top of this mound is slightly dished and mostly covered with gorse.

Frances Lynch (Lynch. F. *A Guide to Ancient and Historic Wales. Gwynedd.* 1995. Page 108.) calls the motte Castell Cynfael and states that it is a castle motte and is known to have been constructed by Cadwaladr in 1147. In fact, the motte is far from ideal as a defensive position, as it would be possible for archers to station themselves at a higher level on the hillside to the south east and fire arrows into the defences, whilst themselves being out of reach of the defenders arrows. It is possible though that Cadwaladr fortified an existing mound, which already had a ditch cut into the solid rock, as this could be done quickly with relatively little effort.

From the O.S. map it appeared that large rocks situated at Castell Mawr (SH 5806 0481), near Llanegryn, would be almost, but not quite, in line with the midsummer setting sun, when viewed from Bryn-y-castell. On visiting Bryn-y-castell it became apparent that the summit of Carn Fadryn, the highest visible point on the Lleyn Peninsula, could be seen a little to the right of the rocks, and would provide a much more likely foresight. In fact no other point on the Llyn Peninsula could be considered to be anything like as satisfactory and at a distance of over 45 km. it would, if in the correct direction, be capable of giving high accuracy. There is no indication at Bryn-y-castell that it was intended as a backsight for solar observations, but such an indication would be unnecessary, as the foresight is quite obvious and the setting Sun, at the summer solstice, would automatically direct the observer in the right direction.

Careful measurements from the O.S. maps and using methods given by Thom (Thom, A. *Megalithic Lunar Observatories* 1971) indicated that the declination of an object setting behind the summit of Carn Fadryn, when viewed from Bryn-y-castell, would be close to 24.288 degrees, which, allowing for the mean semi-diameter of the sun of 0.267 degrees, would indicate a declination for the sun of 24.021 degrees. Photographs of the setting Sun taken from Bryn-y-castell near the time of the summer solstice, 28th June

1976, confirmed that the result could not be greatly in error. This declination is about one tenth of a degree higher than values obtained by Thom for Scottish solar observatories and it corresponds to an earlier date of about 2900B.C.

The declination of the Sun in 1976, when my photographs were taken was 23.255 degrees. In 2900BC it was close to 24.02degrees, which is 0.765 degrees higher. As the diameter of the Sun is close to 0.53 degrees, the trajectory of the setting Sun would have been just over one Sun diameter higher than shown in the next diagram and the Sun would have set squarely against the left hand face of Carn Fadryn.

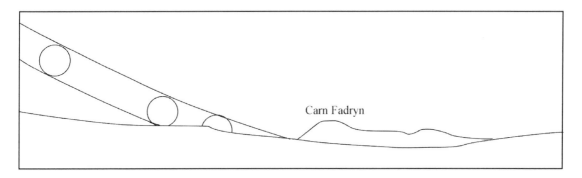

Figure 9.1 Three positions of the setting Sun, derived from photographs taken two days after the Summer Solstice of 1977.

In the days preceding the solstice the Sun would have set more to the left of Carn Fadryn, but by moving up the hillside behind the mound it would have been possible to find a position from which the Sun would have been seen to set exactly against the face of the mountain. As the solstice approached, this position on the hillside would have become progressively lower. After the solstice the observer would have had to retreat up the hill again to see the Sun set in the same position. In this way the site could have been used over a period of several hundred years to find the time of the Summer Solstice.

Just to the right of the summit of Carn Fadryn there is a very small notch and it is possible that the top edge of the Sun could have been glimpsed for a brief period after it had disappeared from sight behind the main mass of the mountain. This would have provided a very sensitive and accurate means of making the observations. Another point of interest is that the azimuth of the upper limb of the setting Sun would have been 313.3 degrees, which means that the Sun would have set almost exactly in the north west.

These observations strongly suggest that Bryn-y-castell formed part of a Solar observatory and it would undoubtedly have worked well as such, but the evidence is circumstantial and without more archaeological evidence of the date of the mound, it is not possible to be certain.

THIRTEEN STONES HILL
THE REDISCOVERY OF A MEGALITHIC RING

In chapter seven, I discussed the name "Thirteen Stones Hill" and wondered if there had ever been a stone circle there. At a recent school reunion I had the chance to find out more, as the Haslingden local historian Chris Aspin was present. He was perhaps the one person who would be aware of any information that was available. He was able to tell me that he was not only aware of the name, but had found a ring of thirteen depressions where stones had apparently stood and had been instrumental in organizing a survey of the site. A copy of the survey had been placed in the public library in Haslingden. He then promised to send me a copy of it, which arrived a few days later. I was also told that from the site, a hill by the name of Hog Lowe Pike, marked the extreme southerly setting point of the Moon and that the midsummer Sun set over the Bleasdale Hills. This was much more than I could have expected.

The plan of the ring was quite large and was on six A3 sheets. Before any work could be done the sheets had to be combined without losing accuracy. This was done by scanning them and combining the results in the computer. In attempting to establish the geometry of the ring I gave more weight to the hollows than the few remaining stones. The ring, as the diagram shows, is very nearly circular, but the north west/south east diameter seemed to be a little longer than the northeast/south west diameter. The best figure I could find which fitted the remains was an ellipse with a long axis of about 88.5 feet and a short axis of 86 feet. These are close to 32.5 and 31.5 Megalithic Yards (32.54my and 31.62my) and are interesting dimensions, as the distance between the foci necessary to give these lengths, has to be exactly 8 my. The total rope length used to scribe the ring would need to be equal to the length of the long axis, that is 32.5 my. The perimeter of the ring, based on this geometry is close to 100.53my. The ellipse superimposed on the plan has these dimensions and has all the properties that Thom described.

In order to fit the remains the short axis of this ellipse must point close to the direction of Hog Lowe Pike and in the other direction to a point between Great Hameldon and Hameldon, hills to the east of Accrington. It must be more than a coincidence that Hog Lowe Pike marks the most extreme southerly setting point of the Moon and the point between the Hameldons marks the extreme northerly rising point of the Moon, when viewed from the ring. For the builders to have found a position, on the highest point of a moor and have accurate sightlines for making two sets of lunar observations, is quite remarkable.

It is often thought that finding the exact position of a sightline for a particular type of lunar observation would have been difficult and time consuming, as it is assumed that the work could only have been done at the times when the Moon had its extreme declination. This however was only true for the establishment of the first such observatory. Sightlines for other similar observatories could be established by observing any star which rose or set over the same sightline and using this star as a guide to find others. For example, if a sightline had been established for observing the rising of the Moon with its extreme southerly declination, then any star which was seen to rise over the same sightline could act as a marker for similar sightlines in other parts of these islands. There would be a small parallax difference if the second observatory were a considerable distance to the north or south of the original one, but it would not be very significant. As there are lots of visible stars, it may have been possible to identify several such stars and if these stars rose at different times of the year, the work of searching could have been extended. When the Moon again reached its extreme southerly declination, the observers would have been be in a position to use any new observatories and perhaps fine tune them, to correct for inevitable errors. If the horizon were low, then due to haze, stars may not have been visible until they had risen a considerable distance above it. This could have caused errors, but it would not have been too difficult to devise approximate corrections. The 18.6 years between these extreme lunar events could have been well used to locate positions for similar observatories in other parts of the country. The climate in those days may well have been better than ours today, but clouds can always interfere with observations and the more observatories there are, the greater the chance that one or more will have clear skies and allow observations to be made.

This ring, sited on the top of a high moor, must have been very impressive. It is quite large and only about one quarter of the two hundred and sixty rings listed by Thom have greater diameters, and of the thirty five elliptical rings, only three have longer main axes. Many of the stones must have been of considerable size as some of the hollows are well over five feet in width. When approached from any direction the stones would have been silhouetted against the sky. No other ring that I know of would have had such an imposing situation.

We do not know why the ring was destroyed. In some areas destruction of rings was carried out by the Church to remove heathen places of worship, but usually the demolition was simply due to farmers, builders or quarrymen using the ring as a ready source of stone, as was done with many stones at the great ring of Avebury. The pity is that we have lost what must have been a very remarkable ring and can only guess at its original appearance. The details that we can glean are due to enthusiasts such as Chris Aspin, M. K. Eckersall and M. Fletcher for mapping the remains and, at least partly, bringing the ring back to life.

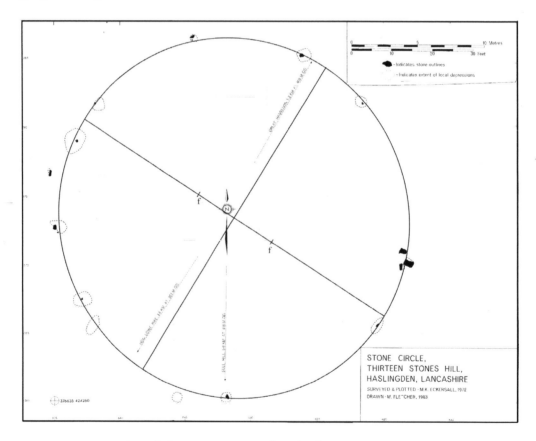

Plan of Thirteen Stones Hill with ellipse superimposed.

Details of the ring:

GR	SD 766 243	Altitude	345m.
Long axis	32.5my.		
Short axis	31.5my.		
Interfocal distance	8my.		
Perimeter	100.53my. (1 my equals 2.72 feet.)		

Chris Aspin also informed me that about three kilometres to the west north-west near Cocker Cobbs there was another stone circle and one five foot long slender stone still remains standing. This was reported to him by Major Halstead, who heard it from his mother. There can be little doubt that stone circles were much more common than is generally realized and we can only study the few that remain. Fortunately there are enthusiasts who do make records of what they have heard and seen about sites, sites that are disappearing at an alarming rate. The difficulty lies in tracking down this information.

SITE OF RING AT THIRTEEN STONES HILL   J.R.H.

A POSSIBLE CALLANISH SIGHTLINE

A recent visit to the standing stones of Callanish proved how easy it is to overlook a possible sightline. The main ring has five rows of stones radiating from it. By standing by the stone at the east end of the eastern row and looking towards the main ring, it was possible to see through a very narrow gap to the distant hill Suainaval, 429m high and 13km distant. A movement of ones eye by only a few centimetres loses the view completely. Thom used this line of stones in the opposite direction, looking east, but did not indicate that it could be used to look west. The stones of this row are not set out on the same straight line, which would not have been too difficult to do, but appear to be staggered, so that some stones are on each side of the presumed sightline. The result is that an apparently ragged line of stones becomes a highly accurate direction finder. The indicated declination is close to -5.6degrees. This declination does not correspond to any of the events considered important by Thom, so, unless it has another use, it is possible that this apparent sightline is accidental.

Possible sightline along the East row looking west.

CHAPTER 10

CONCLUSIONS

Throughout I have attempted to think of the megalithic builders as people who were little different in their basic abilities from people today. Many of their beliefs would no doubt seem strange to us, but I believe that we must regard them as our intellectual equals. There would have been a few highly gifted individuals, but as there were far fewer people in total in these islands than now, there would have only been a small number of them. Perhaps because of that, they would have stood out from the rest and would in suitable societies move on to more influential positions.

There can be no doubt that Neolithic and Bronze Age societies were structured, otherwise large undertakings such as Stonehenge, the Avebury complex and Silbury hill could not have been constructed. What is also clear is that their basic ideas and beliefs were widely disseminated and appeared to have changed little over long periods, as is demonstrated by the building of stone rings throughout the British Isles for a period of well over one thousand years. There were differences however, both over time and from place to place. For example the recumbent stone circles of Northeast Scotland form a group essentially distinct from those of other areas and in general there was a tendency for very large rings to be of an earlier date than smaller ones. The problem is to account for the differences without losing sight of the striking similarities.

Perhaps the peoples of these islands were divided into tribes, each with its own region of influence, but all connected by similar, but not necessarily identical, belief systems, overseen by religious leaders. It would perhaps have been similar to the structure of many present day religions and it is a structure that has proved itself both robust and resilient.

To be a religious leader or priest would be a great honour and presumably there would be competition to be selected, so only outstanding individuals, or members of families of high standing could become recruits. Then there would probably follow a rigorous process of training and learning that would give the newly promoted priest authority and set him, or perhaps her, apart and above the rest of the population.

What exactly these beliefs were is probably beyond our abilities to know, but if there is any validity in the astronomical interpretations of many megalithic sites, then they are likely to have included some knowledge of the movements of the Sun and Moon and probably eclipses. Burl referred to the subject of death and regeneration, and death and rebirth, (Burl *Prehistoric Avebury*. pages 200 to 203) and what more potent symbol of death and rebirth is there than an eclipse? Even today an eclipse of the Moon inspires wonder and a total eclipse of the Sun is awe inspiring (even when hidden by clouds). Anyone able to predict such events would have been thought to have mystical, or even magical powers and perhaps be able to commune with the Gods.

In trying to predict eclipses, it would soon have become apparent that Lunar eclipses take place at the time of full Moon and Solar eclipses close to the time of new Moon. The problem is to find out which full or new moon would result in an eclipse. Once committed to this path of eclipse prediction it would have been natural to endeavour to improve on their predictive ability and this in turn would have necessitated improved observatories and observation techniques. The methods used may well have been secret and not at all obvious to the onlooker, so we today should not be surprised if we have difficulty elucidating the intricacies of their methods. Their observatories would have had to make do with what was available, such as distant hills, hill slopes, dips in the horizon or on occasions man made hill top cairns. The observers would have to know which part of the hill, slope or other feature was important if they wanted the most accurate result. Thom has described in detail how these observatories could have been used and although at first glance the methods appear complex and difficult, their use would have been straightforward to a suitably trained person even though that person may not have fully understood what he, or she, was doing. Today exactly the same is true of driving a motor car, millions do it but few really understand how they work.

Burl in the last chapter of *Prehistoric Avebury* (Burl, *Prehistoric Avebury*, Page 230) sums up the stupendous achievement of the builders of this gigantic complex and states *"After nearly five unbroken centuries of labour the giant monuments were finished, first Silbury Hill, then the sarsen circles, the ditch, the bank, the Outer Circle, the long stretches of the avenues, finally the stone rings of the Sanctuary."* Then he continued *"Twenty generations of men and women had died since the building started and now it was done…"*

Since Burl wrote that, new and more reliable carbon dates have been obtained from deer antler fragments found near the top of Silbury Hill, which date this monument close to 2400B.C. instead of about 2800B.C. so that it is probable that Silbury Hill was the last great undertaking and not the first and it would seem to postdate the pyramids of Egypt. This change in chronology however does not affect the question of what effects this huge effort had on the local population. Did they do the work willingly, or were they coerced? Did they start the project with great enthusiasm and end up being forced to continue? It seems that towards the end of the project burial practices were changing and communal burials were giving way to single burials in barrows and increasingly the bodies were accompanied by rich grave goods, whilst the communal West Kennet long barrow was filled with soil and the entrance closed off with huge stones. These are indications that wealth and power were being concentrated into fewer hands. Did the people perhaps feel betrayed and sidelined by their chiefs and leaders, or did they lose out to other tribes? Life for farmers in Neolithic times was hard at the best of times and the added burden of building these great monuments over periods of hundreds of years could well have had a serious effect, not only on the general health of the population, but on the structure and unity of society. It is easy to imagine a man telling his grandchildren that his grandfather had told him, that his grandfather was one of the workers who actually worked on the building of the first internal great stone ring and yet after all this time the complex was still not complete. He then asks the question "When will it end?" This may have been followed by a comment that the people to the south have done all right with Stonehenge, a much smaller monument. It is easy to see how despair and disenchantment could set in, especially at times when the harvests were poor and diseases struck.

It seems that after all the work of building Avebury and its associated structures, it was not used for very long. We cannot be certain of the reasons for its demise, but possibly the tribes to the south around Stonehenge conquered the area and allowed the massive monuments to fall into ruin. Was it that the people, driven too hard for too long and drained of all energy, has no will to resist? Perhaps we shall never know.

INDEX

Accrington, 97
alignment, vii, 56, 92, 93
Angell, I. O., 14
Arbor Low, 83
Archaeologia Cambrensis, viii, 2, 18, 45
arcs, vii, 1, 7, 41, 42, 73, 75, 80-83,85
Arthog Standing Stones, 6, 40
Aspin, Chris, 96, 98, 99
Astronomy, 38, 53
Aubrey hole ring, 30
Aubrey holes, 26, 85
Avebury, vii, 25, 26, 30, 39, 41, 55, 69, 73-91, 103
Avenue, 85, 86, 103
Backsight, 45, 46, 47, 55, 93
Bar brook, 65
Barclodiad y Gawres, 72
Barmouth, 5
Bedd Arthur, 2, 17, 18
Black Marsh, 64
Bleasdale Hills, 96
bluestones, 68
Brat's Hill, 63
Briggs, Dr. Stephen, viii
Brodgar, ring of, 25
Bronze Age, 67, 101
Bryncrug, 94
Bryn-y-castell, 94, 96
Burl, A., 2, 11, 74, 86, 102

Bushel, Reverend W. Done, 18
Cadair Idris, 92
Cadwaladr, 94
cairn, 45, 46, 48, 49, 53
Cairnbaan, 69
cairns, 2, 46, 68, 69, 102,
calendar, 1, 93
Callanish, 99
Candlemas, 93
Carn Fadryn, 94, 95
Carnbica, 19
carvings, 70, 71, 72
Castell Cynfael, 93
Castell Mawr, 94
Castle Rigg, 25, 64, 66
cattle, 73
Cefn Caer, 44
Cerrig Arthur, 4, 19, 64
Cerrig Arthur, 10, 11, 18
Cerrig Marcholion, 19
chalk, 85
Cocker Cobbs, 99
cockfighting, 51
Cracking the Stone Age Code, viii
Craig y llyn, 5
Creigiau'r Llan, 53, 57, 58
cup and ring marks, vii, 69, 70, 71
cycle, 18.6 year lunar, 38
David Gough, 45

declination, 18, 46-50, 53, 55-57, 93-97,100

deer antlers, 73, 103

design, of rings, vi, vii, viii, 1, 7, 30, 39, 41, 60, 66

ditch, 73, 74, 83, 84, 94, 103

Dyfi, 44

Dysynni, 51

Earth's axis, 48

Eckersall, K, 98

eclipse, 1, 38, 102

egg shaaped rings, vi, vii, 1, 19, 39, 41, 74

Eglwys Gwyddelod, 8, 18, 19, 51-59

ellipses, vi, vii, 2, 9, 12, 14, 16, 18, 20, 40, 41, 74, 96, 97

Elva plain, 26

Euclid, 43

Euler, 37

Farr West, 26

fathom, 26, 28, 29

flattened circles, vi, vii, 1, 2, 5, 12, 19, 24, 29, 36, 40, 60-67, 74

Fletcher, 98

Foel Goch, 46

gangs, of workers, 73, 74

Gauss, 37

Gray Croft, 66

ground penetrating radar, 85

Halstead, Major, 99

Hameldon, 97

Hardy, G. H., 37

Haslingden, viii, 71, 96

Heath, Robin, viii, 41

Higgins, Steven, viii

Hirnant Cairn Circle, viii, 2, 13, 17, 41

Hog Lowe Pike, 96, 97

Hurlers, 26, 28

Ilkley Moor, 71

Irish passage tombs, 71

Kilmartin, 69, 71

Knowth, 71

Large Hadron Collider, 39

Limestone, 83

Llanbrynmair, 11

Llanegryn, 94

Lled Croen-yr-ych, 10, 12, 19, 65

LLeyn Peninsula, 92, 94

Llwyngwril, viii, 92

Long Meg, 65

Lunar measure, 25, 26

Lunar Observatory, vii, 45, 48, 50, 51-59

Lynch, F., 94

Malone, Caroline, 55, 74

Martinmas, 93

Mathematics, 37-43, 82

Megalithic Remains in Britain and Brittany, viii, 14, 85

Megalithic Sites in Britain, 16, 21, 102

Megalithic Yard, vi, vii, ix, 1, 5, 7, 9, 12, 14, 16, 18, 20-30, 40, 41, 75, 84, 96

Moon, 5, 38, 39, 46-50, 53-57, 96, 97, 102

Neolithic, 43, 44, 46, 68, 74, 101, 103

Newgrange, 71

Newham, 25

Nine Stones (Winterbourne Abbas), 16

Obelisk, 55

obliquity of the ecliptic, 53

observatories, vii, 38-40, 46, 94-96, 102

old foot, 24, 25, 30, 75, 85, 91

Old Yard or O.Y., 24, 25, 26, 28, 29, 30, 75, 80, 81, 84, 87

Orkney, 29

outlier, 5, 12, 25, 63-67

Owain Glyndwr, 44

parallax, 46, 48, 53, 57, 97

Pembrokeshire, 69

Pembrokeshire Inventory, 17

Pen Carreg Gopa, 45-49

Pen Creigiau'r Llan, 53, 56, 58

Pennal, 44-50, 51, 53

Prescelly Hills, 69

Pumlumon, 52, 58

Pythagorean triangle, 1, 39, 40, 42, 75, 80, 84, 85

quarry, 68-71

Ramanujan, Srinivasa, 37

recumbent stone circles, 101

right angled triangles, 1, 40, 41, 80, 82

Ring of Stenness, 29

Rings from other sources, 24, 34

Rings of lesser accuracy, 24

Rings, Large English and Welsh, 23, 24, 30

Rings, Large Scottish, 23, 24, 26, 28, 30, 35

Rings, Small English and Welsh, 23, 24, 29, 30, 35

Rings, Small Scottish, 23, 35, 36

Ruggles, Prof. C., 51, 54, 56

sagitta, 42, 82, 83, 91

Sanctuary, 85, 86, 103

Seascale, 66

sightline, viii, 38, 50, 52, 53, 55, 56, 63, 93, 97, 99, 100

skyandlandscape.com, viii

Solar and Lunar cycles, 38

stone fans of Caithness, 40

stone hole sockets, 83

Stonehenge, vi, 25, 30, 39, 68, 69, 72, 85, 101, 103

stones, for rings, 68-72

Suainaval, 99

Sun, 38, 39, 46, 47, 50, 53, 55, 56, 57, 93, 94, 95, 96, 102

Sunhoney, 25

Sylfain, 5

symmetry, of the Avebury ring, 80, 84

Temple Cairn Circle, 15

The Royal Commission for Ancient and Historical Monuments in Wales, viii

Thirteen Stones Hill, 71, 96, 98

Thom, Alexander, vii, viii, ix, 1, 2, 14, 19, 20, 21, 28, 30, 38, 39, 40, 41, 48, 56, 60, 63, 64, 67, 75, 85, 94, 95, 96, 99, 102

Thomas apGriffiths, 45

Tomen Las, 44, 46-49, 53

Tywyn, viii, 51, 94

Waterhouse, John, 64, 66

Waun Oer Alignment, 94, 95